MY
HOPE
is in
YOU

MY
HOPE
is in
YOU

PSALMS THAT COMFORT
AND MEND THE SOUL

BILL
CROWDER

Discovery House.
from Our Daily Bread Ministries

My Hope Is in You: Psalms that Comfort and Mend the Soul

Previously published as *Singing the Songs of the Brokenhearted.*

Portions of chapter 12 were adapted from the Discovery Series booklet *It's Not Fair: Trusting God When Life Doesn't Make Sense* by Bill Crowder © 2003 by Our Daily Bread Ministries.

Discovery House is affiliated with Our Daily Bread Ministries, Grand Rapids, Michigan.

ISBN: 978-1-62707-934-1

Printed in the United States of America
First printing of this edition in 2018

*For those who have influenced me
on the musical journey of life:*

*David Randlett
Clayton Erb
Kerry Wheeler*

Contents

Acknowledgments

I am deeply indebted to so many who have helped and influenced me on my journey. Ed Curtis, my seminary professor in the Exposition of Psalms course at Talbot School of Theology, taught me a rich value for the songs of the Scriptures. My friend and colleague Mart DeHaan has helped me learn and grow in both the craft of writing and in the exercise of critical thinking, a unique and valuable part of that craft—in which I still have much to learn. My parents taught me to love and appreciate music, and to hear behind the notes and words the heart of the music. My friends and brothers in ministry David Randlett, Clayton Erb, and Kerry Wheeler modeled for me how music and worship coordinate, or collide, to impact our hearts by the power of song. It's all good.

As always, I am honored to work with my colleagues at Discovery House Publishers. I want to thank Carol Holquist and the publishing committee for accepting my book proposal; Judith Markham, for encouraging me as I worked to shape and clarify my thoughts and ideas; and to the DHP support posse of Annette Selden, Melissa Wade, Kevin Williams, Katy Pent, Jill Lamberson, and Peg Willison for the spirit with which they approach their work. I am honored to count them friends.

Special thanks to my wife, Marlene, for her patience and understanding as I worked (and worked and worked) on the manuscript. My kids, a wellspring of illustration material, are also deserving of gratitude. They put up with a lot, and I am grateful.

And to my Savior, my gratitude for the song of salvation. "He put a new song in my mouth, a song of praise to our God" (Psalm 40:3). I pray that Christ will help me to sing it well.

Introduction

W hile a student in seminary, I heard a statement that changed forever how I read one of the most significant portions of the Scriptures—the Psalms:

> In the Bible, we have 66 books.
> In 65 of these books, God speaks to us.
> In the book of Psalms, we speak to God.

Suddenly a lot of things fell into place. I had a new perspective on this powerful poetry. To see the psalms as an inspired account of human emotional reaction to the events of life gave context to what I had read and was, at times, troubled by. How can you reconcile the psalmist's heart cry that his enemies' babies be dashed against rocks or for the annihilation of a people group? Suddenly it became clear that God wasn't condoning or endorsing those emotions. His inspired record reveals how deeply our hearts react to the events of life—sometimes rightly and sometimes wrongly, but always reacting.

Bible teachers say that some of the Bible is prescriptive (telling us what to do) and some of it is descriptive (giving us an inspired, factual account of what happened). Using that lens, we see that much of the book of Psalms is descriptive—telling us how real people in real situations displayed real emotions.

And it is encouraging to know that on occasion those emotions led to worship, celebration, and joy.

In this book, however, we want to examine psalms that go the other direction—psalms that deal with life's darker moments and more painful experiences. The emotional responses to those events are decidedly more difficult. But our God preserves them for us—perhaps to let us know that *He* knows the turbulence and struggle we feel in those times. And, in many of those songs, to remind us how wise it is to entrust our pain and problems to Him because He *does* understand.

So I invite you on a journey of the heart: a journey that takes us into the reality of life's greatest challenges, and a journey that takes us to the God who is more than enough to carry us through the difficult seasons of life. These songs are a reminder that followers of Jesus never face these struggles in isolation. God understands—and He is there.

Psalm 6

The Heart Broken by Grief

Grief teaches the steadiest minds to waver.
—SOPHOCLES

One of the most melancholy characters in pop culture has to be Charlie Brown of *Peanuts* fame. He is constantly on the short end of things, with mistreatment coming from every direction. Lucy torments him with alleged psychological insights into his many phobia, and then compounds them by suckering him into kicking the football—only to, inevitably, pull the football away just as he is prepared to kick it. He is dogged by the athletically superior Peppermint Patty, and never quite able to reach the dream of his boyhood heart, "the little red-haired girl." Even his dog Snoopy seems to be superior to him in all things, and isn't afraid to show it. Poor Charlie Brown.

Interestingly, Charlie's default response to the onslaught of life's struggles, disappointments, and failures is to drop his head in despair and mutter, "Oh, good grief."

I can identify with Charlie's frustrations. But the expression that has become his trademark—his kneejerk response to the sadness of life—is one that I find odd. "Good grief" seems to be an oxymoron, a contradiction of terms. *Good* grief? I would suppose that few (if any) grieving people think their grief to actually be good. Grief is something to avoid, not something to embrace. It is something that disturbs life, not something that enhances it.

Ancient Israel's King David, a singer of songs, certainly struggled to see any kind of goodness in his own experiences of grief. Consider his heart cry in Psalm 6:6–7:

> *I am weary with my sighing;*
> *Every night I make my bed swim,*
> *I dissolve my couch with my tears.*
> *My eye has wasted away with grief;*
> *It has become old because of all my adversaries.*

"My eye has wasted away with grief." What a load of pain is wrapped up in those words. That load of pain is what makes grief such a powerful emotional force. In 1970 when the Beatles released the song "Let It Be," the overwhelming assumption was that Paul McCartney was making a religious reference to the Virgin Mary when he sang of "mother Mary" coming to him in his "times of trouble." But it was not a religious icon he longed for; it was his own mother, Mary McCartney, who had died when Paul was a youngster. He missed her. He longed to talk to her when life was filled with pain. His words "Let it be, let it be" speak of the great vacuum left in his life by the absence of the loved and lost. Good grief? Not so much.

Grief Is Personal

During my twenty-plus years of pastoral ministry I spent many hours with families in the darkest moments of life—in surgical waiting rooms, emergency rooms, doctors' offices, funeral homes, and counseling centers. There they grieved over the death of loved ones, illness, broken relationships, the loss of a job, and many other kinds of losses.

Part of what made their grief so brutal is that it is so personal. Even events that are sweeping in scope produce a grief that is deeply personal and felt in the most private ways.

I grew up in West Virginia and was living there in November 1970 when the Marshall University football team, along with coaches, boosters, and community leaders from Huntington, West Virginia, were killed in a fiery plane crash on the hills outside the Tri-State Airport in Huntington. I had gone to grade school with one of the players and had gone to high school with another. It was one of the most heart-rending experiences I had, at age eighteen, ever seen. Yet, as the state of West Virginia and the communities of Huntington and Marshall University mourned and wept, each person involved felt the grief privately. Public outpourings of sorrow over the massive loss of life could not even begin to express the internal pain of each person affected by the tragedy.

In the film *We Are Marshall*, which tells the story of the Marshall air disaster, one of the characters reminds the erstwhile fiancée of his dead son, "Grief is messy." Indeed. It is messy, and it is messy in part because it is so personal, regardless of how public or sweeping the causes of grief may be.

Grief Is Honest

In Psalm 6, there is no indication of the specific cause of David's grief. His pain is real, but he doesn't tell us what its source is. Yes, he does mention the attacks of mean-spirited people that have exacerbated his heartache (vv. 8–10), but they are not the main focus of his psalm. In the very personal depths of his suffering, David's thoughts turn to his disappointment with God.

> O LORD, *do not rebuke me in Your anger,*
> *Nor chasten me in Your wrath . . .*

And my soul is greatly dismayed;
But You, O LORD—how long? (Psalm 6:1, 3)

Honesty is the defining characteristic of the Psalms. In these ancient songs we find honest, gut-level responses to the real-life circumstances of actual human beings—joy, anger, bitterness, guilt, resentment, vindictiveness, and every other emotion that we human beings feel. It is out of the honesty of their emotions that the psalmists express their responses to life.

One of my seminary professors said that in the Bible we have sixty-five books in which God speaks to us, and one book in which we speak to God—the Psalms. And when the psalmists speak to God, they do so without any attempt at religious propriety. There is no attempt to swath everything in spirituality. There is no interest in saving face. There is just honesty.

Here, as David sinks into the depths of his pain, yes, he cries for help from God. But he is crying to a God he thinks has deserted him. In fact, he feels that God is punishing him by bringing this grief upon him. Notice the words he uses to describe the conflict in his heart:

"Do not rebuke me in Your anger, nor chasten me in Your wrath" (v. 1). Whatever else may be involved, David sees his season of pain as the rebuke of God in his life. In his commentary on the psalms, *The Treasury of David*, the great preacher Charles Spurgeon remarked that David is not resistant to God's rebuke, but he does not want to be rebuked in anger. He wants God's rebuke to be formative, rather than punitive, in his life.

"My soul is greatly dismayed" (v. 3a). *Dismayed* speaks of a heart that is vexed, troubled, and deeply disturbed. Spurgeon said of this, "Soul-trouble is the very soul of trouble. It matters not that the bones shake if the soul be firm, but when the soul itself is also sore vexed this is agony indeed."

This is not some superficial matter that David can shrug off easily or quickly. It is a pain that cuts him to the quick. He reaches to his God in the moment of his struggle—but with what result? **"But you, O Lord—how long?" (v. 3b).** Notice that David seems to interrupt his own thought, or cut off part of his intended comment with the phrase, "How long?" as if he is asking his God, "Until when?" His dismay and grief seem multiplied by the sense that he is pouring out his heart to God but hears only silence in return. "How long will I endure with this pain alone?" seems to be at the very heart of his grief.

David doesn't sugarcoat his words or minimize his emotions. He backs up the truck and unloads everything he is feeling on the God that he thinks has abandoned him in his time of grief. He does not identify the cause or source of his grief, but makes it abundantly clear that, at some level, his grief has been compounded by his perception of God's distance from him in his time of need.

Grief Is Painful

> *Be gracious to me, O LORD, for I am pining away;*
> *Heal me, O LORD, for my bones are dismayed. (Psalm 6:2)*

Listen to the words David uses: *pining* and *dismayed*. These are not neutral words. They are powerful descriptions, pregnant with emotion. When he uses the term "pining away," he describes both his emotional and his physical condition. The actual Hebrew term speaks of someone who is weak or feeble. To me, this brings to mind extreme vulnerability, and conjures images from the past.

In my first pastorate, our church held a weekly service at an area nursing home. We would arrive early and go from room to room, inviting the residents to the service, then wheel them out in their wheelchairs or, sometimes, in their beds. These men and women were utterly helpless. They were dependent on the staff and sometimes on visiting loved ones. And, once a week, they were dependent on us. Their feebleness and weakness made them vulnerable. They were "pining away."

"Dismayed" goes even deeper. It is the same term David uses in verse 3, but here he applies it to his bones. One commentary says that King David is telling God that the grief in his heart has shaken him down to his very frame. It is not a light breeze that has drifted into his life; it is a raging storm that has terrified him to his core. It is a *crisis*.

A colleague of mine likes to say that a crisis is any event that forces us to fundamentally reorganize the way we live our lives. Even "good things," such as a wedding or the birth of a child or the start of a new job, can be a crisis because they require a serious depth of restructuring in the way we live. Here, however, David is speaking of a different kind of crisis—the kind that rocks your world and unsettles your heart.

How can such pining and dismay be turned to health and hope? Only by rescue—and there is only one source of rescue.

Grief Longs for Rescue

Return, O Lord, rescue my soul;
Save me because of Your lovingkindness.
For there is no mention of You in death;
In Sheol who will give You thanks? (Psalm 6:4–5)

Here David acknowledges that his pain is too great and his grief too deep for him to be able to handle it alone. He needs help, and only God's help will do. "Return and rescue!" (v. 4) becomes the cry of his heart.

Notice, however, that he is not seeking rescue because he feels he deserves it. He seeks rescue because God is a rescuing God. This is the essence of *mercy*. David seeks what he does not deserve, but what is in keeping with the character of the great God that he still trusts, in spite of his grief. It is a trust rooted in God's *lovingkindness*—His mercy that endures forever (Psalm 136).

David implies that he will openly praise God for His rescue by declaring that he cannot give praise in death, only in life. But the appeal is the same: "God, please, rescue me!"

Grief's Deep Response

I am weary with my sighing;
Every night I make my bed swim,
I dissolve my couch with my tears.
My eye has wasted away with grief;
It has become old because of all my adversaries. (Psalm 6:6–7)

Here, at the core of his song, David's anguish takes full voice. Notice that he unveils how his grief has become all-consuming, manifesting itself in four ways:

Fatigue

"I am weary with my sighing" (v. 6a). The burden of grief may be invisible, but it is exceedingly heavy. It saps the energy from a person, causing a weariness that is draining. Contributing to that fatigue is the simple reality that people battling grief cannot seem to stir up an appetite, which results in a lack of nourishment that exacerbates the physical weariness.

In my years as a pastor, I was always moved by the practical caring and generosity of people who brought food (casseroles, bread, cakes, salads) to the home of the grieving, even though I knew that in the midst of grief most did not want to eat. Beyond that, you don't even feel like you *can* eat.

Also, in times of grief it is difficult to sleep because your dreams are haunted by words and deeds that somehow interact with the grief. All of this creates a weariness, a fatigue, that is precisely what David is describing. Of all his needs, food and rest are among them.

Tears

"Every night I make my bed swim, I dissolve my couch with my tears" (v. 6b). It is in the darkness, after others have gone their way, that the private expressions of grief take form, which is another reason sleep eludes us in times of grief.

When years of cardiovascular problems finally won and my father's life was taken by the last of numerous heart attacks, his death created a crater in my mother's life that could not be measured. My parents' marriage was a partnership like few I have ever seen. They did everything together. In fact, I never saw my mom drive until after Dad's death. She had never needed a driver's license because they did everything together. They went everywhere together. They were inseparable. Even later, after years of "getting over it," Mom told me that there were still times when she cried herself to sleep. In the privacy of her bed, she could weep without having to give explanations or receive well-intentioned but futile comfort. Her tears were salve for her soul.

Sorrows

"My eye has wasted away with grief" (v. 7a). The idea of the phrase "wasted away" is that of failing, and it is usually connected with old age. Here, however, aging is not the issue. It is grief and sorrow that have dimmed David's eyes, and he cannot see clearly through the dark lens of his heartache. This may even speak of his judgment being clouded by his emotions, because, in a state nearing depression, he is not seeing with clarity and accuracy the situations that surround him.

Fears

"It has become old because of all my adversaries" (v. 7b). David's enemies have worn him down. Some speculate that he was referring to adversaries that were spiritual in nature, such as sin, temptation, Satan, and guilt; but it is more likely that these enemies were human foes.

As we will see throughout this book, David continually faced opposition. It seems, in fact, as if he never had a moment's relief from those who wanted to destroy him. Few of us will ever have that level of animosity directed at us on a continual basis, eroding our hearts and hopes like dripping water eventually wears away solid stone. But in those times when we do encounter mean-spirited people who want to do us harm, we may get a glimpse into David's struggle. Whether from King Saul, or Saul's family, or a once-dear friend (Ahithophel), or even people within his own family (Absalom), there seemed to be no end to the enemies David accumulated throughout his life.

Fatigue. Tears. Sorrows. Fears. This is what makes grief so tough. It engulfs us and taints every moment of life.

Commentator Derek Kidner said this of David's condition: "Depression and exhaustion as complete as this are beyond self-help or good advice. Even prayer has died away. The *foes* who would normally have roused David only crush his spirit now. If anything is to save him it will owe nothing to his own efforts" (*Psalms 1–72*).

Grief of this magnitude feels inconsolable, and, perhaps even worse, inescapable. Our response to our grief drives us to the private agony of spirit that seems to have no remedy—unless we see the only way out: the way of trust.

The Confidence of Faith

The way of trust—that is where David's heart now turns. Notice that his situation has not changed, nor has his grief: "The Lord has heard the voice of my weeping" (v. 8). But what has changed is that he no longer feels abandoned by God. Quite the opposite: "The Lord has heard . . . the Lord receives . . ." (vv. 8, 9). David senses the trustworthiness of the rescue and care of the God who answers his prayers, even in the midst of his grief and pain. It is his confidence in a present reality that impacts his long view of life, and his attitude in it all.

David may have learned this lesson from the experiences of Job. Suffering in ways most of us cannot begin to imagine, Job was overwhelmed by his confidence in the God of heaven. His words express a heart that was learning to trust God—not in spite of his pain, but in the midst of it.

"Though He slay me, I will hope in Him." (Job 13:15)

"As for me, I know that my Redeemer lives, and at the last He will take His stand on the earth." (Job 19:25)

"I will *hope* . . . I *know*." Those words of confident hope—of faith—expressed by Job echo in the words of David the king as he turns from his grief and to his God.

The Present Trust

Depart from me, all you who do iniquity,
For the LORD has heard the voice of my weeping.
The LORD has heard my supplication,
The LORD receives my prayer. (Psalm 6:8–9)

David tells his adversaries that God is still with him, in spite of the struggles he is facing. He is still weeping. He is still feeling the depths of his pain. But he no longer feels abandoned. He recognizes that the God who loves him also hears his prayers—and those prayers matter to Him! Three times David affirms his confidence in a prayer-hearing God, and rightly so.

God does not always answer our prayers in ways that we understand, but He always hears our cries. He does not turn His back on us or ignore us. He is not too busy to listen. He is never disinterested.

What begins to bring peace to David's heart is the confidence of faith: that God is listening to the tear-stained cries of his grief.

The Future Hope

All my enemies will be ashamed and greatly dismayed;
They shall turn back, they will suddenly be ashamed.
(Psalm 6:10)

In the final stanza of his song, David moves beyond his present struggles to the anticipation of victory to come. The present tense of verses 1 through 9 anticipates the future exoneration in verse 10, and the day is won.

When we are consumed by the grief of today, it is difficult to remember the promises of tomorrow that we have from the Father. In the upper room, the night before Calvary, Christ could sense the grief in His disciples at their coming separation from Him. What was His response to that present reality? Look ahead! He said: "Therefore you too have grief *now*; but I *will* see you again, and your heart *will* rejoice, and no one *will* take your joy away from you" (John 16:22, emphasis added). The present *now* of their grief is answered by the future *will* of seeing Him and rejoicing with an eternal joy!

It is an amazing thing to see grief turned to hope, loss turned to anticipation. It is a transformation of heart and spirit that brought David to a confident trust in the ways of a God he didn't claim to understand. He only claimed to believe.

The same was true of Christian businessman Horatio G. Spafford, who experienced his own Psalm 6 season of grief.

Spafford was a lawyer whose real estate holdings were destroyed in the Great Chicago Fire of 1871. Also, his only son died about that same time. For two years after the fire, Spafford, a friend of evangelist D. L. Moody, helped many of those made destitute by the fire. At that point, he decided to take his wife and four daughters on a holiday to Europe. Stafford was delayed by business, so he sent his family on ahead. Tragically, the ship on which they were sailing collided with another vessel. His wife survived, but all four of his daughters were lost. Later, this grieving father and heartbroken believer expressed his own confident trust in the God whose ways are past finding out as he penned these words:

> *When peace, like a river, attendeth my way,*
> *When sorrows like sea billows roll;*
> *Whatever my lot, Thou hast taught me to say,*
> *"It is well, it is well, with my soul."*

It is well with my soul. To be able to say those words in the extremities of grief and loss is an amazing thing. Yet Spafford understood what David many centuries earlier had sung about: even in our grief, God cares and comforts. He loves and listens. Our grief matters to our God, and knowing that brings hope.

Purposeful Grief

When my dad passed away in 1980, I had been a full-time pastor for a grand total of two days. His funeral service would be my first. For the previous nine months, my wife and I had commuted each weekend to my hometown from the Bible college where I was teaching in order to help plant this new church ministry. Dad had been an integral part of that, and we had talked almost every weekend about how things would be once I was on site and we could work together. My first Sunday, however, Dad had a massive heart attack and two days later was in the presence of his Savior.

One night at the funeral home, as I was standing by the casket during the visitation time, a pastor friend came and quietly stood by me. After a few moments of silence, he softly said, "One day you will be thankful for this."

Thankful? I thought. *You must be crazy!* The look I gave him must have telegraphed what I was thinking because he put his hand on my shoulder and explained his words.

"I have been a pastor for many years and have performed dozens of funerals. But I have never lost anyone close to me. I still have my parents and uncles and aunts. I am thankful for that. But I also know that I have never been able to look into the eyes of a grieving family and say, 'I know how you feel.' You will be much better equipped to minister to hurting people because of what you are feeling right now."

Although I didn't recognize it at the time, my friend's words were prophetic. In my years of pastoral ministry, funerals became a rich time of sharing and caring for others, and those seasons of grief became deeply meaningful times of ministry. In fact, my wife, Marlene, has often joked that when I die my tombstone should read, "He did good funerals and weddings."

Good grief? I'm not sure Charlie Brown's catchphrase is the best or most helpful response. I think a better phrase might be "purposeful grief." If we can learn to allow our grief to have purpose—to inform our living and loving and serving—then our own moments of sorrow can prepare us for great opportunities for spiritual impact, which is what Paul was calling us to when he wrote:

> *Blessed be the God and Father of our Lord Jesus Christ, the Father of mercies and God of all comfort, who comforts us in all our affliction so that we will be able to comfort those who are in any affliction with the comfort with which we ourselves are comforted by God. (2 Corinthians 1:3–4)*

May His comfort in our grief move us to comfort others.

Psalm 12

The Heart Broken by Despair

More than any other time in history, mankind faces a cross-roads. One path leads to despair and utter hopelessness. The other, to total extinction. Let us pray we have the wisdom to choose correctly.
—WOODY ALLEN

S ome songs are just troubling. I remember, as a teenager in the summer of 1966, waiting with great anticipation for the release of the newest Beatles album, *Revolver*. I brought it home, put it on the big Motorola stereo in our living room, and started to listen. Much of it was good, fun, standard Beatles fare. Then I heard the haunting "Eleanor Rigby." I was unprepared for the song and for the impact it had on me. It filled me with sorrow. The beauty of the double string quartet accompaniment gave an air of elegance to the song, but the grandeur of the music could not offset the deep sadness of the words. "All the lonely people, where do they all come from?" The anguished voice of multitudes of heartbroken people seemed gathered up into that painful lament. A woman living and dying without hope . . . a minister functioning and serving without purpose. Even today it remains one of the saddest songs I have ever heard.

But soon after that the boys from Liverpool released another song that eclipsed "Eleanor Rigby" for sheer heartache. On their vaunted *Sergeant Pepper's Lonely Hearts Club Band* album, amid songs both fanciful and provocative, fun and psychedelic, the

Beatles strategically placed a song of pure and utter despair. "She's Leaving Home" tells the story of a young girl who quietly gets up one morning, packs a few things, and runs away from home, "leaving a note that she'd hoped would say more." She was looking for love and excitement and breaking her parents' hearts in the process. The cries of the girl's parents revealed an inconsolable anguish. Losing a child is, after all, a pain beyond measure.

The idea that music can express our emotional highs and lows, that lyrics can capture the despair of the hurting heart in a unique way, finds support in the fact that the Hebrew hymnal, the book of Psalms, contains so many laments. Or consider the prophet Jeremiah, who wrote an entire book of such songs called Lamentations. The emotional gravity of the despair of life sometimes calls not for a sermon, but for a song—and Psalm 12 is just such a song.

Here, David looks at the struggles facing those who seek to live for God in a world that sees no value in such a commitment. He sees a world in opposition to all he believes, and feels the enemy is winning. He sees a world filled with oppression, and aches for those who are oppressed. Surrounded by hearts failing under the pressure of living faithfully, David angrily seeks God's vengeance on those who are causing him pain. Somehow, it seems a song of despair is all that is left for a heart lamenting a world gone terribly wrong.

The Despair of the Faithful

Once again, it begins with fatigue. As I think about that word, I think about my recent ministry trip to Asia when, after two weeks of travel and teaching, I contracted some kind of stomach bug. But the root of my problem wasn't the stomach virus. It was that, after thirty hours of travel from the States to Singapore, I had to immediately get on another plane to another country and then jump headlong into teaching ministry without giving my body time to rest. The fatigue of travel made it difficult for my body to fight off the bug. Instead of letting my body recuperate, I made the choice to drive forward and as a result I eventually had no choice—I was forced to spend a day in bed and recover.

We often underestimate the impact of our physical well-being upon our emotional and spiritual well-being. I know that I do. When we are weary, we don't have the energy we need to face life's pressures, disappointments, or trials. It begins with fatigue—and impacts everything else.

From the beginning of Psalm 12, I think it is evident that David is tired. He is worn out and worn down by life, and by trying and trying and trying—but never seeming to ever get anywhere (like Eleanor Rigby). David knew how it felt to try his best, to be committed to doing right, and to feel nothing but the sharp end of the stick for his troubles. Yet he refused to bottle up those feelings and put on a happy face. He refused to hold it all in and pretend that all was well. David vented his heart—and, when he did, he vented at God himself.

Help, Lᴏʀᴅ, for the godly man ceases to be,
For the faithful disappear from among the sons of men.
(Psalm 12:1)

David knew the frustration of continually struggling for a goal that never seemed to get any closer to his reach. He knew what it was to live in hard times, when living in faith was a target for hate rather than a badge of honor. Matthew Henry, in his classic commentary, wrote this of the times of frustration and despair David described in Psalm 12:

When piety decays, times really are bad. He who made man's mouth will call him to an account for his proud, profane, dissembling, or even useless words. When the poor and needy are oppressed, then the times are very bad. God himself takes notice of the oppression of the poor, and the sighing of the needy. When wickedness abounds, and is countenanced by those in authority, then the times are very bad.

Trying and failing. Seeing the continuing corruption of society and knowing he was powerless to slow its destructive march caused David to recognize that, as Henry said, "the times are very bad." Notice how he described the discouragement of heart that was afflicting him:

"Help, Lord." In his weariness and despair, David cries to God for help. In this moment, he would likely have appreciated the words of the old gospel song, "Where could I go, oh, where could I go? Where could I go but to the Lord?" Where else *could* he go? His only help is in the Lord he has chosen to live for, in spite of the animosity of the world. Like Peter sinking into the waters of the stormy Galilee, David has but one place he can turn, and he calls out, "Help, Lord!"

"The godly man ceases to be." David's fear? That there is a day coming when there will be no godly men or women left to pursue the things of God and to live in His wisdom. David fears an end to the age of the worship of God, and he mourns over such a possibility.

"The faithful disappear." The word *faithful* speaks of those who are grounded and firm in their trust in God. David sees a lack of confidence in God among his people, and he fears that such trust may disappear altogether.

The despair in David's voice reveals the agony of spirit that comes from constantly seeing the deterioration of his generation and pushing back against it, but to no avail—of striving but never reaching, of trying but never succeeding. Commentator John Gill speculated that this struggle may have been the by-product of David, as a young man in the court of King Saul, seeking to live with integrity in the midst of courtiers and sycophants who lied to the king about David and sought his death, or that it could be a reference to the days when his own son Absalom turned on him, seeking to depose David from the throne. In either case, David sees in his own heart a desire to live for God honorably, yet that desire is in danger of being overwhelmed by the duplicity and hate that surrounds him. It is simply wearing him down.

The story of Sisyphus echoes this frustration in an ancient cautionary tale. In Greek mythology, Sisyphus was the legendary founder of Corinth who offended Zeus, king of the gods, and was sentenced to spend eternity pushing a giant boulder up the side of a mountain. He would roll it up the mountain, only to see it roll down again just as he reached the pinnacle; he then had to push it back up again, only to see it roll down again— an endless process. Sisyphus' punishment became a proverb of endless frustration and utter pointlessness.

David had experienced his own temporal version of this mythical struggle and had, at last, been broken by it. He had wearied himself in the noble cause of seeking to honor his God, only to see the crushing boulder of evil come crashing back down. To perpetually try and consistently fail is a debilitating experience. It leads to a despair that Shakespeare described as "past hope, past care, past help."

The Self-Deceit of Wrongdoers

I seldom watch the news on television anymore. Instead, I get the information I need off the internet, where I can filter out what isn't pertinent. For me, watching the news is too depressing. I grow weary of hearing a never-ending litany of the wicked things people do to each other—sometimes in the name of politics, sometimes in the name of religion, sometimes even in the name of love. People hurting others and enjoying it. Random acts of violence. Intentional acts of ruthlessness. Deceitful acts of manipulation. Self-seeking acts of destruction. I just get tired of seeing that day in and day out, ad infinitum, ad nauseam.

The film *Wyatt Earp* follows the life of the legendary lawman of Dodge City and Tombstone, whose exploits at the O. K. Corral became a defining moment in the wild west of the late 1800s. Early in his life, as his family was traveling to California, young Wyatt witnessed his first shooting when he went into a town to buy supplies. Two men gunned each other down in the street, and the boy was sickened by what he saw. Wyatt's father used this gut-wrenching experience as a learning opportunity in his young son's maturing process. It was a lesson about the dark side of human nature, as his father explained, "You know, this land is full of people doing wicked things to each other . . . There are plenty of men who don't care about the law. Men who'll take part in all kinds of viciousness and don't care who gets hurt. In fact, the more they get hurt, the better."

"The more they get hurt, the better." That kind of evil is as brazen as it is ruthless, and over time it develops an arrogance that feels it can do whatever it wishes with impunity. David recognized that arrogance in the overwhelming tide of evil that he saw sweeping through his day—in actions, attitudes, and speech.

They speak falsehood to one another;
With flattering lips and with a double heart they speak.
*May the L*ORD *cut off all flattering lips,*
The tongue that speaks great things;
Who have said, "With our tongue we will prevail;
Our lips are our own; who is lord over us?" (Psalm 12:2–4)

"Who is lord over us?" they ask. Wow! These people flaunt their wicked intentions so boldly that they feel absolutely no accountability for anything they do. They have become experts in falsehood and flattery, and they trumpet their ability to use and abuse their words to accomplish their evil desires in the world. But above and beyond all of that is their thorough disregard for a God who values truth and who holds men and women responsible for how they use or abuse that truth.

Communication is a precious privilege that allows us to meaningfully connect our hearts to the hearts of others, and it is not something to be used as a weapon. But those who want to take advantage of others find words to be just another resource in their tool chest to be used to manipulate, misdirect, or misinform. The sad thing is that each time people use words to trick someone into what they want, these individuals or groups devalue not only their victims but themselves. They think they are deceiving others, and they may even think they are deceiving God, but in reality they are only deceiving themselves:

- Deceiving themselves into believing that it's okay because everyone does it.
- Deceiving themselves into thinking that no one will really get hurt.
- Deceiving themselves into thinking that it doesn't really matter.
- Deceiving themselves into thinking God doesn't see.

But how we use or misuse speech is a huge issue, for if we lose our integrity we lose something that is virtually impossible to regain. And that is just as true of cultures as it is of individuals. At the heart of the Nazi party's rise to power in 1930s Germany was their ability to control and manipulate information in order to control and manipulate people. By shaping people's thinking, the Nazis were able to shape the culture to accomplish their ends.

That is a dangerous thing indeed. Proverbs 23:7 warns, "For as he thinks within himself, so he is." The manipulation of the truth impacts the thinking of people, which impacts the values they embrace and the choices they make, which ultimately impacts the kind of people they actually become—shaping the character of the people and defining the character of the culture.

David saw something similar in his day. Deceiving and being deceived had become a method for advancing evil, and he mourned the devastating effect of deception by self-deceived wrongdoers on his culture. Frankly, I struggle to understand which is worse, the intentional misrepresentation of truth, or the cavalier and uncaring way in which it is done.

The Response of the King

There is only one answer to such despair, and that is *justice*.

Justice is proclaimed as one of the core values of our society—a society built on, as the Pledge of Allegiance declares, "liberty and justice for all." The 1950s television series *Superman* declared that even "this strange visitor from another planet" was the champion of "truth, justice, and the American way." In fact, justice was such a vital concern to our founding fathers that James Madison wrote in the Federalist Papers, "Justice is the end of government. It is the end of civil society. It ever has been, and ever will be pursued, until it be obtained, or until liberty be lost in the pursuit."

The reality, however, is that we live in a world that is filled with injustice. In fact, we live in a world where justice itself is flawed, and in danger of becoming an archaic concept. The concept of justice appears to have been replaced by a justice system that struggles to carry out its overwhelming task. In our day, justice has become more of a punch line—an object of scorn—than a cultural priority. No wonder comedian Norm Crosby once offered this take on the justice system of our day: "When you go into court you are putting your fate into the hands of twelve people who weren't smart enough to get out of jury duty." A far cry from "truth, justice, and the American way."

In contrast, *The Online Dictionary* defines *justice* as "The quality of being just; fairness. The principle of moral rightness; equity. Conformity to moral rightness in action or attitude; righteousness. The upholding of what is just, especially fair treatment and due reward in accordance with honor, standards, or law."

Justice is supposed to be a fair shake—equity of treatment to all regardless of social standing or economic clout. Unfortunately, justice is a tough needle to thread, in part because we just aren't very good at it. At some level, I suspect, this is because of who we are as human beings. We aren't very skilled in the area of administering justice. We tend to excel at revenge, not justice. Often, our pursuit of justice isn't as much about equity and fairness as it is about exacting the necessary pound of flesh so that I feel better about the situation, whatever it might be. In the mad dash of self-interest we inevitably supplant justice with caste systems, declaring with our words that all are equal, but revealing with our actions that some are more equal than others. This is why we must constantly be taking the injustices of life and releasing them to God, confident that the Judge of all the earth will do what is right.

David had been laboring under a despair of heart that threatened to undo him. He saw injustice all around him in the mistreatment of the weak, and declared that they deserved their day in court. He took the evil that men do, the deceptions that men promote, and the injustices that men afflict on others, and released them. Instead of allowing his despair over these things to fester in his heart, poisoning his life, David took all those injustices and turned them over to the Lord of life who answers that justice will be done.

> "Because of the devastation of the afflicted, because of the
>   groaning of the needy,
> Now I will arise," says the LORD; "I will set him in the safety
>   for which he longs."
> The words of the LORD are pure words;
> As silver tried in a furnace on the earth, refined seven times.
> You, O LORD, will keep them;
> You will preserve him from this generation forever. (Psalm 12:5–7)

Notice how God responds to the despair of the faithful. He is not indifferent to the despair of His children. Rather, He sees the "devastation of the afflicted" and He hears the "groaning of the needy." And He is determined to see justice done on behalf of the weak. This nets out into two clear ideals that bring encouragement to David's heart, and hope to those who bear the brunt of men's injustice—and to those who inflict that injustice on others.

The Clarity of God's Perspective

No one is getting away with anything. God sees what is happening and assures the sufferer that the actions and evil of wrongdoers will be met with eventual, if not immediate, justice. What strikes me about this is the personal nature of God's response. "Now I will rise," says God. He responds ("now") to the oppression of the weak He sees on the earth. He rises because He hears the "groaning" (crying, sighing, lamentation) of the needy. God declares that He sees the yearning of their hearts for safety in a dangerous world and He rises to replace the threat of injustice with that very safety.

In part, this Divine insertion, in which God rises to place himself in the equation of evil men and their helpless victims, is hinted at as an ultimate (even if not always immediate) result of the cross. Yet, to our surprise, the suffering of Christ is not limited to the victims of wrongdoing. It is a sacrifice offered for all, victor and vanquished alike.

First Peter 3:18 assures us, "For Christ also suffered once for sins, the just for the unjust, that He might bring us to God, being put to death in the flesh but made alive by the Spirit" (NKJV). Since "all have sinned and fall short of the glory of God" (Romans 3:23), all suffer under the condition of the unjust heart. All need to be brought to God. *All.* So God rises to remedy our unjust hearts with the offering of the Just One, Jesus. In Christ, God has risen, just as He had promised.

The Purity of God's Promise

What a difference this promise is from the manipulation of information by evil men to accomplish their selfish ends! God sees truth for what it is—pure. And David celebrates this purity by describing it as a precious thing, like silver.

As valuable as it is innately, silver's value increases with its purity. David describes a process of refining silver in an earthen furnace where the superheated fires burn away any impurities in the metal, bringing it to its highest possible value. He then declares that God's words are so pure—so devoid of any deception or self-interest—that they are like silver that has been refined seven times. With such absolute purity comes reliability. We can trust God's promises because His words are untainted by the corruption of men.

God's promise of justice was clear from the beginning, and as David saw his nation wallowing in injustice, he must have hearkened back to the words of the Pentateuch: "Cursed is he who distorts the justice due an alien, orphan, and widow." (Deuteronomy 27:19). As a result, David raises his voice in praise as he considers God's assurance of ultimate justice.

Hope for justice is the response of the king of Israel to the response of the King of Heaven to the injustices of this world. Reassured, David now knows that his fears are unfounded. The faithful will not disappear. The worship of God will not be driven out. The weak will not be afflicted forever. God will rise up, and when He does, justice will "roll down like waters and righteousness like an ever-flowing stream" (Amos 5:24).

David's weary heart has been strengthened by the promises of God. He has been reenergized by the prospects of justice for the weak. He has a restored hope in his faithful God. Hope has overcome his despair.

The End.

Well, not exactly. Frankly, I wish the psalm *had* ended with that strong statement of trust and confidence in God's protection of the faithful in verse 7. It would have been a much happier conclusion to this song of despair. But life doesn't always have a happy conclusion, and neither does Psalm 12. It has one more verse.

The wicked strut about on every side
When vileness is exalted among the sons of men. (Psalm 12:8)

After David's chorus of praise, these words seem to ring with the same despair with which the song started. It is a stark conclusion to a troubling song. As in "Eleanor Rigby" and "She's Leaving Home," there is no happy ending—only the reminder that we live in a fallen world that seems to manufacture despair as its primary export. The arrogance of wrongdoers has not been wiped from the earth. Unjust men and women are everywhere.

Yet David has learned one thing: He does not have to be ruined by despair. He must see life as it is, but must also see God as greater than anything life can throw at him.

When we witness injustice and evil in the world, when we are the victims of deception and manipulation, when we are tempted to succumb to despair, we can have hope. God has promised that, in His own time, He will deal with the injustices of this world. We can believe that promise, with hope in the Christ who has come as the ultimate, matchless fulfillment of God's promise. A hope that hymn writer Norman J. Clayton described beautifully:

My hope is in the Lord
Who gave Himself for me
And paid the price of all my sin at Calvary.

For me He died;
For me He lives,
And everlasting life and light He freely gives.

Psalm 13

The Heart Broken by Defeat

There are some defeats more triumphant than victories.
—MICHEL DE MONTAIGNE, 1533–1592

F ew times in my life have I been more apprehensive or more nervous than the days I was the starting goalkeeper on the varsity soccer team of our Bible college. It was the first year of our soccer program and most of the players, like me, had very little experience playing the game. Most of us were washed-up football players who weren't good enough to earn scholarships but still wanted to play sports. Soccer beckoned, we came running, and our coach had the thankless task of trying to whip us into something resembling a soccer team. His theory? What better way to learn than from the best! We discovered this, when he shocked us with the news that he had scheduled us to play against Howard University in Washington, D. C.

Howard was not another small Christian college. They were the defending national soccer champions. The week before our match with them, Howard had defeated a school with an established, respected soccer program by a score of 16-0. So the question was not whether we would lose; the question was whether we could limit their scoring to less than a hundred!

But part of our coach's theory was that there were worse things than losing. Among those "worse things" was "not learning." He believed that losing to the best collegiate team in the country would teach us more about the game of soccer than a dozen wins against mediocre, or less than mediocre, teams. He was more concerned with building our abilities than feeding our egos. Defeat was to be seen as an educational opportunity, not just a number in the loss column.

In Psalm 13, we come upon King David following one of his experiences of defeat. It appears that David wrote this song of grief after his son Absalom turned on him and drove him from the kingdom. In the backwash of that reversal of fortune, David, overwhelmed and destitute, turns to God as his only resource in his dark days.

The Self-Examination of Defeat

Abraham Lincoln was one of America's greatest and most beloved presidents. He freed the slaves and saved the republic, but those great victories stand in stark contrast to his early political failures. Jan Jacobi, of Clayton, Missouri, in a February 11, 2000 commentary in the *St. Louis Post-Dispatch*, described Lincoln's failures this way:

> At each stage of his life Lincoln knew failure and defeat.
>
> In his twenties, Lincoln struggled with identity issues. By studying grammar and reading extensively, he acquired knowledge and discovered the rhythms of language. In speeches before the New Salem debating club, he honed his orator's voice. In the law and in politics, he found the vehicles through which his passion could be engaged and in which his talent could emerge.
>
> But against this backdrop of self-discovery came discouragement and failure. He lost his first job, as clerk in Denton Offutt's store, when Offutt's business enterprises collapsed. Lincoln and Berry, a successor store, failed,

leaving the partners in debt. If we give moderate credence to the tale of Ann Rutledge, he was unlucky in love.

In his first campaign for the state Legislature, he placed eighth among thirteen candidates. In a campaign document, he had stated that if he were to lose, he "was too familiar with disappointments to be very much chagrined."

The middle period in Lincoln's life was spent in Springfield. There he became a successful lawyer and made a brief foray into national politics. He still faced identity issues. Abruptly, he broke off his engagement to Mary Todd and, as a result, experienced a profound depression. The core of it was the failure of will that he saw in himself. Helping his friend Joshua Speed deal with similar apprehensions about marriage, he rallied, and a year later reconnected with Mary.

After his term in Congress, his political career languished. The Kansas-Nebraska Act in 1854 galvanized him into action, but in 1855 and 1858, he experienced two bitter defeats in contests for the Senate. In the 1855 campaign, he came agonizingly close to victory. Lincoln coveted a Senate seat. It was where he saw himself serving most effectively as the country polarized in the late 1850s. In early 1860, when his name first surfaced as a presidential possibility, Lincoln did not think he was qualified.

According to the historical record, Lincoln followed those times of failure with a serious season of soul-searching. Defeat does that to us. Certainly in today's culture, where blame-shifting is one of the favorite indoor sports, we often follow our seasons of failure with a careful study of who else we can blame for our shortcomings. Eventually, however, most of us are forced to look within, forced to reckon our own contributions to our defeats. We must face the facts and accept our weakness, in essence forcing ourselves to see what everyone else already knows. Whereas in brighter days we too often find ourselves warmed by the sun of our own abilities, in times of somber reflection following defeat we are often driven to God. David's defeats caused him to do precisely that:

> *How long, O LORD? Will You forget me forever?*
> *How long will You hide Your face from me?*
> *How long shall I take counsel in my soul,*
> *Having sorrow in my heart all the day?*
> *How long will my enemy be exalted over me? (Psalm 13:1–2)*

As David faces the reality of his defeats, he is forced to examine himself and to ask himself some tough questions.

Questions about His God
"How long, O LORD?"
"Will You forget me forever?"
"How long will You hide Your face from me?"
David feels that he has failed to the point where even God has given up on him. Like David, many of us wonder if God cares about our struggles, or, in our worst moments, we wonder if He is there at all. Like David, in the midst of our loss we find ourselves asking over and over, "How long, God? How long?"

To think that you have been forgotten by God is a terrifying thing. And for David, it is a place he never thought he would find himself. He has fallen far and hard from his days as a trusting shepherd boy with seemingly boundless faith.

Questions about Himself
"How long shall I take counsel in my soul, having sorrow in my heart all the day?"

David looks within, and sees a heart wracked with sorrow. Even worse, he sees a heart that he no longer trusts. His choices and decisions have produced this failure, and his confidence is gone. He knows his perspectives have been badly skewed by life's failures, particularly his failures with his son Absalom. (He would mourn that rebellious son in days to come, but he would also mourn his own failings as a father.)

Questions about His Opposition

"How long will my enemy be exalted over me?"

In effect, he is saying, "This defeat is real, and those who have beaten me down are enjoying every moment of my humiliation." The enemies that have brought David such anguish seem to live by the motto, "It's not enough that I succeed—everyone else must fail!" Life has become a zero-sum proposition. Not only are they celebrating their win, they are basking in the glory of David's loss. For David, the shame and disgrace of his defeat is only amplified by the way his foes are lording it over him.

David's defeats have brought him low. So low, that he is now beginning to ask questions that are more than sorrowful lament; they are questions that reveal how delicate his faith has become. This kind of self-scrutiny is neither pleasant nor easy. David sees what he has become—and it breaks his heart.

The Heartache of Defeat

Cinderella Man, one of my favorite movies, tells the true story of James J. Braddock of New Jersey, the "Bulldog of Bergen." Once a heavyweight boxer who aspired to the championship crown, Braddock saw his reversal of fortune begin with the onset of the Great Depression. Like countless others, he lost everything he had amassed during his years of success. Then his career was torpedoed when, desperate for income, he had no choice but to box with a hand that had been broken and was not yet healed.

Destitute, he sought work on the docks but could never get enough income to stay ahead of the bill collectors. Devastated by his inability to care for his family, Braddock finally surrendered his pride and signed up for welfare assistance. But even that was not enough to pay the bills. What could he do? He couldn't afford food, heat, or any of the other basics of life needed by his wife and children.

In the film inspired by Braddock's life, this crisis sets the stage for one of its most poignant scenes. It is a moment that reveals the depth of a heart broken by defeat. Braddock returns to Madison Square Garden, the scene of so many of his boxing victories, and walks into the club where the sports reporters, boxing moguls, and bigwigs spend their days. Apparently untouched by the ravages of the Depression, they look down their noses at the once-proud fighter in the ragged clothes of a common laborer. In tears, Jimmy takes off his hat and begs for money.

It is difficult to put into words the fear parents experience when they don't know how they will be able to care for their family, for those they love. It is a personal failure that cuts to the bone and to the heart. You don't simply want to die; you feel as if you might as well already be dead. David felt that as well. He felt the burden of unmet expectations and cried to God for help.

> *Consider and answer me, O LORD my God;*
> *Enlighten my eyes, or I will sleep the sleep of death,*
> *And my enemy will say, "I have overcome him,"*
> *And my adversaries will rejoice when I am shaken.*
>   *(Psalm 13:3–4)*

As David considers the impact of his failures and the reach of his defeat, he cries out to God because of the depths to which he has fallen. Once mighty and powerful, he is now struggling to survive.

"I can't find the light—enlighten me!" In those moments of humiliating failure, something snaps within us. We crave isolation, preferring the painful solitude of darkness to the bright companionship of friends or family. We crave solitude, because it seems that every face reminds us of our failure. That every word is somehow a jab at our defeat. Everything around us is a loud, though silent, rebuke of our inabilities. We want nothing more than to crawl into the dark so that we don't have to face anyone in our shame. We can't find the light, even as we somehow know that we desperately need it. It is a terrible place to be.

"I fear death is imminent—the sleep of death!" I find David's phrase, "or I will sleep the sleep of death" interesting, because I suspect that he does, in fact, fear death, but also, deep down, welcomes the escape death offers. In that sense, the "sleep of death" implies rest from the weariness of his struggles, and the assurance that all his sorrows, trials, and failures in this life will be over at last. Perhaps, like Elijah in the cave at Horeb or Jonah under the shady plant at Nineveh, David looks at his life and sees nothing worth continuing. His recent failures now loom so large in his mind that perhaps he believes his life itself has been a failure and that the only solution to that harsh reality is death.

"I am rattled by my failures—I am shaken!" While David's enemies are happy about his failures, David is shaken by them. Sometimes, this distress is a result of lofty expectations that are rooted in earlier success. We have succeeded before and, therefore, assume that future success is assured—but it isn't. And, when, in the midst of those expectations, our efforts fall short, it can be extraordinarily disturbing. We wonder, "How could this have happened? I don't understand. How can this be?"

David's words reflect the bleak feelings of a man who is on the threshold of depression. Notice how this very real condition is described on a website dedicated to the struggle faced by people who battle with it:

> Some people say that depression feels like a black curtain of despair coming down over their lives. Many people feel like they have no energy and can't concentrate. Others feel irritable all the time for no apparent reason. The symptoms vary from person to person, but if you feel "down" for more than two weeks, and these feelings are interfering with your daily life, you may be clinically depressed. ("Depression Basics," www.depression.com)

Depression terminology did not exist in David's day, but the experience did. And the once victorious soldier and beloved king now struggles to identify what he can do to reverse the devastating effects of his defeat.

The Thrill of Victory

On June 9, 2007, Simon Cowell, of *American Idol* fame, was one of the hosts/judges of a similar talent show in the United Kingdom called *Britain's Got Talent*. I first heard of it when my sister Carole sent me the web link to an online video clip from the show. "You just *have* to watch this clip—it's extraordinary," she wrote in her attached email. I clicked the link and prepared to see some terribly bad singer make a fool of himself or herself.

The clip showed a somewhat round, ordinary looking chap— a mobile phone salesman—who seemed awkward and very much out of place on stage. When asked what he was there to do, he nervously replied, "I'm here to sing opera." The judges looked at one another skeptically—one even appeared to smirk at the thought that this phone salesman could pull off any musical piece, let alone Puccini's "Nessun Dorma."

The music began and the phone salesman, still looking very nervous, opened his mouth and began to sing. And what followed was truly magical. He sang with the grace and power and ability and freedom only known by those who feel they have nothing to lose. People in the crowd began nodding their appreciation, then some began to weep, then even the judges were caught up by the magic of the moment. Before the man could even finish the power crescendo that would conclude the piece, the crowd was on its feet cheering wildly.

The shy man with the grand voice was Paul Potts, who went on to win the entire competition. Today, he travels the world singing opera, living the dream for all those who have tried and failed, or, for fear of failure, never tried at all.

David also experienced the thrill of victory as he rose from the ashes of defeat to a new hope and a fresh faith.

But I have trusted in Your lovingkindness;
My heart shall rejoice in Your salvation.
I will sing to the LORD,
Because He has dealt bountifully with me. (Psalm 13:5–6)

This is what Erwin Lutzer, pastor of the Moody Memorial Church in Chicago, is driving us to grasp in his little book *Failure: The Back Door to Success*. Lutzer reminds us of one of life's most valuable lessons—the same lesson our soccer coach was trying to teach our team. Failure and defeat are usually hard, never fun, and sometimes painful, but they are not without value. They are, as one pastor put it, the bumps of yesterday that we will climb on tomorrow.

David now puts things into the harsh, but wiser, context of lessons learned. He balances the past with the future, all the while understanding that we can only live today. See how David puts these things in perspective in verse 5 and 6:

Past	Future
"I have *trusted in Your lovingkindness"*	*"My heart* shall *rejoice in your salvation"*
"He has *dealt bountifully with me"*	*"I* will *sing to the Lord"*

It is a wonderful thing to see David learning from his defeat. It is even more wonderful to see him connecting the faithfulness of God to his anticipation of a brighter day, particularly since he was questioning that very faithfulness in the early portions of this song.

In a sense, by balancing past and future, David is going back to his youth. Here, David does something similar to his actions on the day he came to the encampment of the Israelite army and found them in a standoff with the Philistines (see 1 Samuel 17). Goliath of Gath, a nine-foot-tall warrior, was challenging Saul and his soldiers to send a champion to fight him on their behalf. No one would volunteer for what seemed to be a suicide mission until the young shepherd, David, volunteered.

The first response to his offer was mockery, and David explained the reason for his confidence. While shepherding his father's flocks, on separate occasions David had to face a lion and a bear, each looking for a quick snack at the expense of one of David's sheep. In each confrontation, David defeated the enemy—but he made it clear that his victory was not by his own strength:

And David said, "The LORD who delivered me from the paw
of the lion and from the paw of the bear, He will deliver me
from the hand of this Philistine." And Saul said to David,
"Go, and may the LORD be with you." (1 Samuel 17:37)

This boy, who was too small to even be able to wear proper
armor, based his confidence in future victory on God's past
record of faithfulness.

Now, years later, David finds that this is still a good strategy for facing the challenges of life. He looks back in order to
look ahead. His confidence for better things to come is firmly
rooted in his past experience with the God he is learning to
trust once again.

David recognizes that God's provision of yesterday offers
hope for tomorrow, and he is determined that the songs of
celebration he has sung in the past will become, once again, his
anthems of praise in the future. This doesn't change the reality
of his present, but it offers hope at a time of desperate need.
And sometimes even a little hope is enough.

A Change of Perspective

We lost that soccer game against Howard University. In fact,
we didn't just lose, we got creamed, 8–0. Howard took some
50 shots on goal, and we took some 50 fewer shots than they
did. That's right. We never even got off a shot. Brutal.

On the other hand, we saw the beautiful game of soccer
being played the way it should be played. And we saw it from
a vantage point that no amount of game film could have ever
provided. We had the opportunity to have another vantage
point as well—the vantage point of allowing our future choices,
blessings, challenges, and experiences to be informed and edu-
cated by our past defeat.

This is the upward reach of faith in the gloom of defeat—an upward reach that puts our struggle into context and brings light into our darkness. Perhaps it was just such a reality that the Christian recording artists Casting Crowns had in mind when they sang of praising God in the storms of life. For He is who He is, no matter where we are.

And perhaps after all, this is the key: David's situation hasn't changed, but his perspective has. All because the lessons he has learned in defeat are no longer seen as the end, but as the opportunity for a new beginning in his walk of faith with God.

Of all the lessons life teaches, perhaps the lessons of defeat teach us best because they so thoroughly get our attention and so unrelentingly hold on to it. There, in our own cave of defeat, we learn, like David, that it is always too soon to quit—and that God is still in control, even when life feels like it is out of control. The kind of experience Bible teacher and pastor Alexander Maclaren described as "A very threadbare lesson, but needing to be often repeated."

Psalm 32

The Heart Broken by Guilt

Guilt is anger directed at ourselves—
at what we did or did not do.
—PETER MCWILLIAMS

I n 1997, I was in Moscow to teach at the Moscow Theological Institute. The years of Communism had driven the church underground so thoroughly that, when freedom came, not only was there a lack of trained pastors, there was also a lack of people who were trained to train pastors. As a result, pastors and teachers from the West were being invited to teach those interested in serving in ministry. For me, it was a revelation. To see and be with men and women who had suffered so much, and were still suffering, brought perspective to the challenges that I was facing at the time. I had been sent to teach, yet I was learning far more than I could ever convey to them.

One of the most profound lessons I learned was about the power of love and the power of guilt. Admittedly, this seems an odd pairing, but it was the point of the lesson nonetheless.

Since most of the students lived outside the city of Moscow and were living subsistent lives, I thought it might be fun to give them (27 in all) what I thought would be a treat. I told them we would ride the subway to the station at Pushkin Square and I would treat them to dinner at McDonald's. In those days in Moscow, families would save for an entire year just to make one trip to the Golden Arches. It was more than a meal; it was the promise of a dream—a dream of the kind of freedom and prosperity that the West takes for granted. It was a treat these students could never afford, but one that I was sure they would long remember.

The next afternoon, only hours before we were going to make our way to the land of Big Macs and milkshakes, the two class leaders came to my room and asked to talk. After a few moments of awkward silence, the class president said that the class had discussed it at length and did not feel that they should go to McDonald's. Their reason was a mixture of love and guilt—how could they enjoy such an extravagance when their families had little or nothing to eat back in their villages? As much as they appreciated the offer—and loved the idea—they just couldn't go. After a brief discussion, we agreed that the money that would have been spent on burgers and fries would instead be used to buy each man a bag of groceries to take home to his family. It was a significant and moving moment for me—and an educational one.

Guilt, whether motivated by love or by shame, is a powerful reality that can instruct us if we will let it. We can learn the value of making wise decisions and the danger of making foolish ones. We can learn to be moved by the priority of relationships and to be concerned about how our actions can impact those relationships. Guilt has the power to teach and it has the power to destroy—sometimes a razor's edge of difference. The power of guilt to break a heart can also be the power to heal that once-broken heart, and that is the lesson that the poet-king of Israel teaches us in Psalm 32.

Some see Psalm 32 as one of two penitential psalms (along with Psalm 51) that form David's expressions of repentance over his sin with Bathsheba (see 2 Samuel 11). Bible teacher J. Vernon McGee, however, disagreed. He chose to include Psalm 32 in the wisdom psalms because it gives valued instruction about our relationship with God. Whichever way you view it, this psalm makes it clear that there is wisdom in repenting of sin rather than seeking to avoid its consequences by trying to cover up our guilt.

In relating his own shameful experience, whatever that experience was, David is telling us that God will discipline His children if we set out on the wrong road. God's purpose in the pain, however, is not simply to punish. It is to have us make progress on the right way—His way—and His methods of discipline will always be appropriate for the task.

David, having responded to that discipline with repentance, declares the wonder of forgiveness, but also encourages the reader to see sin and deal with it, rather than waiting for God's discipline. "Learn better than I did!" David cries.

Looking for Happiness

In Derek Kidner's commentary on the Psalms, he begins his examination of Psalm 32 with the question: "Happiness is . . . what?" A fascinating question. What is happiness? What does it really take to be happy? Have you ever found yourself saying, "I could really be happy, if only_____." How would you fill in the blank?

Happiness is finding real love.
Happiness is having a full bank account.
Happiness is moving up the corporate food chain.
Happiness is a nice house.
Happiness is the latest electronic gizmos.
Happiness is breaking 80 on the golf course.
Happiness is _____.

David learned the hard way that the key to happiness was not to be found in the "now" things—temporal things of life that do not touch the eternal. David certainly was no ascetic, nor am

I. I believe that God provides countless opportunities for us to appropriately enjoy and celebrate life. And David doesn't deny that. But he does say that true abiding happiness comes in building and maintaining a close, strong, and growing relationship with the heavenly Father—and sometimes that depth of relationship can only be accomplished by dealing with the guilt in our hearts.

This concept of relationship is clearly expressed in the Scriptures in two ways:

- The Positive—A life that is marked by obedience to God: "Where there is no vision, the people are unrestrained, But happy is he who keeps the law" (Proverbs 29:18).
- The Negative—A life that is guilty of disobedience against God, but has been restored: "Behold, how happy is the man whom God reproves, So do not despise the discipline of the Almighty" (Job 5:17).

In Psalm 32, David also expresses the significance of rightness with God both positively and negatively. At the beginning of the psalm, he gives a summary as he wraps his thoughts around several key words in verses 1–2:

How blessed is he whose transgression is forgiven,
Whose sin is covered!
How blessed is the man to whom the LORD does not impute
iniquity,
And in whose spirit there is no deceit!

Blessed

Blessed is an exuberant word, comparable to *happy* or *joy-filled*. Clearly this is the meaning that caused Kidner's "Happiness is . . ." question, and it continues the chorus struck in Psalm 1:1:

How blessed is the man who does not walk in the counsel of the
   wicked,
Nor stand in the path of sinners,
Nor sit in the seat of scoffers!

In Psalm 1, the blessed man or woman is blessed due to spiritual stability. Here, in Psalm 32, the blessed man or woman is blessed due to restoration from spiritual instability. This reflects afresh the wisdom of Proverbs 28:13, which states:

He who conceals his transgressions will not prosper,
But he who confesses and forsakes them will find compassion.

This has been David's experience, and the release from guilt has become the source of his joy.

Forgiven/Covered

Here the psalmist paints two distinct images of forgiveness. One pictures the lifting of sin from us ("forgiven"), and the other pictures the concealing of that sin from God's sight ("covered"). These images combine to describe the biblical concept of justification.

The New Testament doctrine of justification speaks of what God does to place us in right relationship with himself by removing the hindrances of sin and guilt to that relationship. The apostle Paul reminds us, however, that this rightness with God can only be accomplished through Christ's work on the cross: "Therefore, having been justified by faith, we have peace with God through our Lord Jesus Christ" (Romans 5:1).

Impute

David develops that theme of restoration further when he shifts from imagery to serious theology as he uses the word *impute*, which means "to place to someone's account." This is the same concept we find in Paul's discussion of reckoning in Romans 4:6–8:

Just as David also speaks of the blessing on the man to whom
God credits [reckons] righteousness apart from works:

"BLESSED ARE THOSE WHOSE LAWLESS DEEDS HAVE
BEEN FORGIVEN,
AND WHOSE SINS HAVE BEEN COVERED.
BLESSED IS THE MAN WHOSE SIN THE LORD WILL
NOT TAKE INTO ACCOUNT."

When God treats us as if we are righteous, He is dealing with us in a manner that is beyond what we deserve. It is not an earned reward. It is a gift offered in grace and received by faith. The sincerity of heart expressed in the latter part of Psalm 32:2 removes the possibility of abusing that gift by sinning willfully against the grace of God.

In justification, God has imputed righteousness to us. He has forgiven us and placed "right standing with Him" in our account! And the condition for that forgiveness is our sincere repentance. As one Bible teacher said, "Repentance is more than informing God about sin. It is agreeing with Him about that sin and turning to Him from the sin." It is Peter, in Luke 5, seeing the identity of Jesus revealed in His power, displayed in the miraculous catch of fish. In the presence of the power of God, Peter suddenly comprehends his own personal sinfulness and, falling on his knees, says to Christ, "Go away from me Lord, for I am a sinful man!" (v. 8). Without that real understanding of his heart's true condition, Peter would have never been able to respond to Jesus' call, "Do not fear. From now on you will be catching men" (v. 10). When we acknowledge our sin and embrace grace, we find ourselves liberated from the slavery of guilt.

The simple reality is that repentance turns a life around. For the wonderful work of grace in our lives, God deserves the response of obedience from His child. David understood that, and gives us his account of how it felt to be disciplined for his sinful disobedience.

Feeling the Weight of Guilt

In the film *The Last Samurai*, Captain Nathan Algren is celebrated as a hero of the Civil War as well as the wars against the Indian tribes of the Great Plains. But Algren does not feel like a hero. He is haunted day and night by the memories of his actions in those conflicts. Participating in the senseless slaughter of entire villages—women, children, and the aged—might have been lauded by the public and honored by his superiors, but Algren felt no honor. Only shame. He did not feel heroic. Only guilt. As a result, Captain Algren becomes an alcoholic, so consumed by his guilt for his actions that he has become a pathetic shell of a man, unable to function.

In John Bunyan's classic allegory *Pilgrim's Progress*, Christian labors under a similar load—the burden of personal sin. As he makes his way to the Celestial City, Christian faces doubt, despair, legalism, and morality, but none can relieve him of the burden he carries. Unlike Algren, however, who found only futility in his attempts to escape his guilt through alcohol, Christian finally arrives at the place of deliverance, the only place guilt can be truly relieved—the cross and empty tomb of Jesus Christ. There, Christian's burden falls off, and his guilt and sin are finally gone.

The burden of guilt is a load we are not capable of carrying, and it will destroy us under its weight if we seek the wrong sources of relief for that burden. Psalm 32 confirms that King David learned this truth the hard way.

The Extent of God's Chastening

David's initial reaction to his guilt was a common one: He responded with silence and unrepentance. But God knew the truth about David's heart, and so did the psalmist's conscience. David's silence resulted in God's active chastening in his life, which affected him physically, emotionally, and spiritually. Notice his vivid description:

> When I kept silent about my sin, my body wasted away
> Through my groaning all day long.
> For day and night Your hand was heavy upon me;
> My vitality was drained away as with the fever heat of summer.
> (Psalm 32:3–4)

Poetry uses words to paint pictures, and the picture David paints here is not rendered in pastels or bright, vivid colors. On the contrary, he selects dark, somber hues.

The word translated here as *body* signifies a person's bones, representing one's whole physical structure and essence—even the person himself. To say that the bones are "groaning" expresses depth of suffering, for the word speaks of inward grieving and sorrowing. The point here is that David's suffering was *not* superficial. He was literally weakened physically by his refusal to repent and the resulting load of guilt that he was carrying.

In addition to the depth of David's grief, however, is the duration of it. He says that it continued "day and night." As bad as the guilt was, the fact that it was inescapable only compounded it. Why? Because he was continually feeling the pressure of God's "hand," the poetic rendering of divine pressure to deal with guilt instead of hiding it. This pressure reflects the biblical warnings:

> "But if you will not do so, behold, you have sinned against the Lord, and be sure your sin will find you out." (Numbers 32:23)

Do not be deceived, God is not mocked; for whatever a man sows, this he will also reap. For the one who sows to his own flesh will from the flesh reap corruption, but the one who sows to the Spirit will from the Spirit reap eternal life. (Galatians 6:7–8)

It seems that this is a new experience for David, who has repeatedly known the hand of the Lord in blessing or directing or empowering. Now, he feels the heavy hand of the Lord in rebuke, and the result is a kind of personal spiritual desert. David says his "vitality" is being drained from him by the intensity—"the fever heat of summer"—of God's pressure. What a graphic description of the suffering David endured because of this divine chastening! This may be descriptive of a physical illness accompanied by a burning fever as the instrument of the Lord's chastening. But whatever form it took, to David, God's discipline was like the hot, arid Mediterranean air that depleted the region's plants of their inner moisture. What a contrast to the blessed man, planted by the waters the psalmist described in Psalm 1:3.

We see a similar situation in Paul's letter to the Corinthian church. In 1 Corinthians 11:20–34, Paul gives the church family instructions on how to celebrate the Lord's Supper. It is a celebration that the congregation at Corinth had been abusing by making it an opportunity to divide the church family into "haves" and "have nots" (v. 22). The love feast had become an opportunity to advance self and honor pride, rather than a time to focus the attention of one and all on Christ's sacrifice. What they were doing might seem minor to us, but it was not minor in the eyes of a holy God. God's response to their abuses? "For this reason many among you are weak and sick, and a number sleep" (11:30). Things that we might wink at, God takes seriously—and works in our lives to teach us the destructive nature of those inappropriate choices, actions, and attitudes. It is not punishment for punishment's sake; it is discipline for correction's sake, and it demands a response.

So, with God's hand of discipline on his life, how did David respond?

The Extent of David's Response

As he feels the heat of conviction upon him, David's response is not automatic; but when it finally comes about, it is genuine.

I acknowledged my sin to You,
And my iniquity I did not hide;
I said, "I will confess my transgressions to the LORD";
And You forgave the guilt of my sin. (Psalm 32:5)

David no longer attempts to gloss over these things. Instead he acknowledges his sin and is prepared to receive the consequences. He repeats this theme when he uses the word *confess*, which in its New Testament context means "to say the same thing." It means that there is no more equivocation, no more rationalization, and no more self-excusing of his actions. He now sees his wrongful behavior the same way that God sees it, and it is a view that drives him to his knees in confession.

Like the Prodigal Son who came to himself in the pigsty and said, "I will get up and go to my father, and will say to him, 'Father, I have sinned against heaven, and in your sight'" (Luke 15:18), David now turns to God—not as the source of his grief but as the source of his relief. As David declares in another of his songs, "As far as the east is from the west, so far has He removed our transgressions from us" (Psalm 103:12).

In his classic hymn "It Is Well with My Soul," H. G. Spafford's words not only trumpeted his confidence in God during a season of grief (see chapter 1), but also declared the exuberance of profound rescue and liberation:

> *My sin, oh, the bliss of this glorious thought!*
> *My sin, not in part but the whole,*
> *Is nailed to the cross, and I bear it no more,*
> *Praise the Lord, praise the Lord, O my soul!*

To be brought to the point where David now finds himself is a painful process indeed. Yet it is well worth it to sense and know the joy of spiritual restoration.

It is all about a loving Father who cares enough to discipline His wayward child, and the description of that discipline is critical. The Hebrew word for *discipline*, which is used frequently in Proverbs, is clear in its purpose. The methods of discipline may vary, but the purpose and goal are always the same: to correct wrong behavior so that we can have the joy of rightness with God. As the writer of Proverbs wisely reminds us, the hard way of wisdom is still superior to the easy path that brings only death.

Embracing God's Protection

The connection is clear. When David was protecting his sin, he was placing himself outside the protective care of obedience. Now, with restoration to God realized, he sees how desperate life becomes when it is lived away from God's presence.

> *Therefore, let everyone who is godly pray to You in a time when*
> *   You may be found;*
> *Surely in a flood of great waters they will not reach him.*
> *You are my hiding place; You preserve me from trouble;*
> *You surround me with songs of deliverance. (Psalm 32:6–7)*

David now offers the wise counsel gained from his own experience. He wants others to benefit from it as well, and so he calls all who hear his song to "pray to you [the Lord]" so that they/we might know the safety of turning to God and from sin, rather than experiencing the necessary consequences that wrong choices and actions produce. In essence, David says that we have two options:

Option 1: "A flood of great waters"
This is an image of calamity, perhaps the calamity that is the byproduct of poor choices, or perhaps that which is a result of chastening. It may even be that David wants the listener to remember the flood of Noah which came about as a direct result of the sins of humanity.

Option 2: A "hiding place"
This is a favorite expression in the Psalms for God as our shelter from trouble when the enemy encompasses us.

In a stopover in Amsterdam, en route to Israel for a study tour, the group I was leading had a lovely day tour of the Dutch capital. While there we visited the Corrie ten Boom house, where she and her family protected Jewish citizens from the Nazis during World War II. Our guide gave us some interesting history on the family, then took us to the compartment they had built into one of the rooms of their home—a compartment they called "the hiding place." It was an indescribably moving experience to crawl into that space where so many had been protected from death.

David, too, found his hiding place of safety—in his God. And God is our hiding place as well. This does not imply an absence of troubles, but of God's protection in the midst of life's troubles. When those troubles come, He is the one who surrounds us with "songs of deliverance." What an encouragement!

These songs of rescue are God's tender reminders of His faithfulness in our seasons of distress. Charles Wesley, the brother of John Wesley and the poet-laureate of the Great Awakening, emphasized this in the lyrics of one of his great hymns:

Jesus, lover of my soul,
Let me to Thy bosom fly,
While the nearer waters roll,
While the tempest still is high.
Hide me, O my Savior, hide
Till the storm of life is past;
Safe into Thy haven guide;
O receive my soul at last.

The point here is not that we should always escape heartache and trial, but that we should discover what generates those difficulties and what our resources are in them. The person who tries to live on his or her own terms can only turn inward, in a misguided attempt at self-protection. But the child of God can turn to Him and know His preserving care in the midst of the direst circumstances.

Growing in Grace

The apostle Peter wisely instructed the early followers of Christ to "grow in the grace and knowledge of our Lord and Savior Jesus Christ" (2 Peter 3:18). Growing in grace is a life journey that comes with hills and valleys, with sunshine and storms, with joy and pain. All along the way, however, all of the above, and countless more life experiences, provide the instruments through which God does His shaping work in our lives and through which He helps us to grow in grace and in Christ.

David sounds this same note as out of his experience of sin and guilt, of confession and restoration, he closes his song by offering three principles that are part of the journey of growth and spiritual formation in our lives.

The Principle of Instruction

The clearest and simplest way to avoid chastening is to pay attention to the Lord's instruction. Here, the Lord himself is speaking to David (and to us). He promises to guide us with the information we need to make the right choices in life:

> *I will instruct you and teach you in the way which you should go;*
> *I will counsel you with My eye upon you. (Psalm 32:8)*

Talk about instruction! When God himself is our teacher, we know that His wisdom flows out of His deep love for His child. His Word can be trusted, not only because it is true, but because it is born out of God's desire for us to truly experience the wonderful abundance of life that Jesus came to provide (John 10:10b).

The Principle of Submission

When Christ confronted Saul of Tarsus on the Damascus Road, He said to him, "It *is* hard for you to kick against the goads" (Acts 9:5 NKJV). Saul was doing himself great harm by resisting the instruction of the Lord. David felt the same way:

> *Do not be as the horse or as the mule which have no*
>   *understanding,*
> *Whose trappings include bit and bridle to hold them in check,*
> *Otherwise they will not come near to you. (Psalm 32:9)*

While the first principle deals with recognizing the wonder of the God of the universe offering to be our Tutor for life, the second deals with the attitude in which we respond to that tutelage. The challenge here is significant. It is the need for a teachable spirit, one that humbly accepts and responds to the Lord's instruction. The writer of Hebrews understood this well, writing:

*And you have forgotten the exhortation which is addressed to you
as sons, "*MY SON, DO NOT REGARD LIGHTLY THE DISCIPLINE
OF THE LORD, NOR FAINT WHEN YOU ARE REPROVED BY
HIM; FOR THOSE WHOM THE LORD LOVES HE DISCIPLINE,
AND HE SCOURGES EVERY SON WHOM HE RECEIVES.*"*

*It is for discipline that you endure; God deals with you
as with sons; for what son is there whom his father does not
discipline? (Hebrews 12:5–7)*

Sometimes God must use the tools of force to break the
stubborn or obstinate spirit, but He uses these harsh methods
to keep us from destroying ourselves. And His discipline is
purposed by the truest of love.

The Principle of Faith

But ultimately the question will come: Why should I submit
to the Lord's instruction? Why should I obey His Word? And
this is the response that issues from the heart that believes:

Many are the sorrows of the wicked,
But he who trusts in the LORD,
lovingkindness shall surround him. (Psalm 32:10)

The meaning of the Hebrew word *trust* is confidence, security,
even boldness. And therein is the difference between the life of
those David calls "the wicked" and the person he himself wants
to become. His confidence must turn from himself to his God,
for he now begins to see just how inadequate he is to deal with
the pressures and temptations of life. David embraces in principle
what Paul would write centuries later, "Not that we are sufficient
of ourselves to think of anything as *being* from ourselves, but our
sufficiency *is* from God" (2 Corinthians 3:5 NKJV).

What a contrast David highlights here, between the sorrows of the wicked and the assurance of the Lord's love and

mercy to those who place their confidence in Him. And what will be the result?

> *Be glad in the* LORD *and rejoice, you righteous ones;*
> *And shout for joy, all you who are upright in heart.*
> *(Psalm 32:11)*

Notice that David does not promise wealth or health or prosperity. He promises the joy of the Lord, which no circumstances destroy. And that returns us to where David began this song, with what it means to be *blessed*. He reminds us that even as we journey through the darkness of guilt and the struggle of correction, we are going somewhere. We are being drawn to live closer to and walk closer with the God who wants us to be blessed and to know joy, as Jesus said in John 15:11: "These things I have spoken to you so that My joy may be in you, and that your joy may be made full."

What is happiness? Gladness, rejoicing, and joy. I feel confident that David, having survived the storms of guilt and correction, would have agreed.

Psalm 39

The Heart Broken by Fear

I knew a man once who said, "Death smiles at us all.
All a man can do is smile back."
—MAXIMUS DECIMUS MERIDIUS, GLADIATOR

W hen I was a kid I was something of a daredevil, unafraid of risks or consequences. Call it the hubris of youth, or call it stupidity, but not much scared me. In our neighborhood we were surrounded by woods filled with grapevines, and we all assumed we were the next Tarzan. So we spent our summer days swinging on the grapevines and jumping from ridiculous heights, never once thinking we might get hurt. Our house was near the top of a hill that was a half-mile high, and in the wintertime we would ride our sleds down the icy street, dodging cars, delivery trucks, dogs, and people alike. I climbed trees and built tree-houses in absurdly high treetops. I even had sleepovers in those tree-houses, though they were nowhere near sturdy enough or safe (they were not exactly built to code). I broke multiple bones playing sports, both organized and unorganized (or disorganized). I know that I must have terrified my parents. What was I thinking?

The fact is, I wasn't. When you're young, you feel invincible. Life stretches before you without limits or limitations. Then you grow up, physically, mentally, and emotionally. You have responsibilities—studies or training that you have to complete, a job or a career, perhaps a spouse and then children, a house, and on and on. Now you have to be ready for the inevitabilities of life that require things like insurance and investments and savings accounts. You start to see life as increasingly fragile and dangerous, and you begin to hedge your bets. You begin to look for safe ground, when years before you would just "go for it." This awakening vulnerability is a pretty unsettling thing.

In part, that is why I found myself intrigued by a particular song by recording artist Five for Fighting. That name itself is intriguing. It seems to imply that this is a quintet, but in fact it is one guy, John Ondrasik, backed by a revolving door of backup players. Five for Fighting? It's a reference to a hockey penalty (five minutes in the penalty box for fighting). Beyond the clever name, however, is the music—thoughtful, contemplative, serious. Especially true of all that is, arguably, FFF's most significant piece to date, "Superman (It's Not Easy)," which speaks of the frailty and weakness of even a superhero when facing the dangers and pressures of life in this complex modern world.

Making the song even more interesting is that it came out a few months prior to the September 11, 2001 terrorist attacks. At its first release it didn't do much, but the song was embraced following those attacks as a lament of, among other things, the ultimate weakness and failure of human strength. The world's only superpower, which days before had felt invulnerable, had been brought to its knees by a handful of terrorists with box cutters. Where once America had felt untouchable, it now felt threats on every side. This sudden sense of vulnerability and mortality was a raw nerve touched by the anguish of a Superman who likewise felt overwhelmed. In Ondrasik's song, he says men weren't meant to soar through the clouds. And we're all searching for a dream.

FFF's Superman discovered what all of us learn sooner or later—life is dangerous. We are *not* bulletproof, and apparently the only things that really are certain are "death and taxes." After all, even Superman was vulnerable to kryptonite. Sooner or later, we all must face the fact that we are mortal.

It is this foreboding sense of his mortality that has gained the attention of the psalmist in Psalm 39. Once again the psalmist is David, and once again his heartbroken reaction is believed by some Bible scholars to be a response to his son Absalom's rebellion. This time, however, David feels that his life is in such jeopardy that his remaining days may be few. The weight and burden of this sense of the inevitability of death has taken his heart to a place of despair.

The Power of Fear

The early days of 1933 were among the bleakest in the history of the United States, for they were overshadowed by the dark storm clouds of the Great Depression. Some 13,000,000 people were unemployed, and the nearly complete failure of the banking system had crippled a nation that just a few years before had been dancing its way vigorously through the "roaring twenties." During this time of national collapse, a new president was elected, one who knew what it was to be handicapped. Leading the nation from his wheelchair, Franklin Delano Roosevelt recognized that the greatest failing was not of the economy. It was a failure of courage.

For that reason, on March 4, 1933 as he delivered his first inaugural address, President Roosevelt called the citizens of the U.S. to look fear in the eye and refuse to blink. He declared: "So, first of all, let me assert my firm belief that the only thing we have to fear is fear itself—nameless, unreasoning, unjustified terror which paralyzes needed efforts to convert retreat into advance."

"The only thing we have to fear is fear itself." Those words marked the new president's commitment to reject the debilitating, paralyzing power of fear and mobilize the nation to renew what it had lost. It was a stirring challenge then. It still is. Fear is the overwhelming enemy of our hearts and spirits.

In a sense, David had been immobilized by his fear. Like a soldier caught between friendly troops and enemy lines, he couldn't move in either direction for fear of being killed by soldiers on both sides. Notice in the opening verses of Psalm 39 how fear has immobilized David, capturing his weary heart:

> *I said, "I will guard my ways*
> *That I may not sin with my tongue;*
> *I will guard my mouth as with a muzzle*
> *While the wicked are in my presence."*
> *I was mute and silent,*
> *I refrained even from good,*
> *And my sorrow grew worse. (Psalm 39:1–2)*

His Declarations

David begins this song by affirming his ongoing belief in his convictions—a belief that demands moral responses. He is determined to display integrity. He recognizes that his enemies are about him, and this has made him see wisdom. He has become circumspect in how he reacts and in how he expresses those reactions. He has set a guard on himself, so that:

"I may not sin with my tongue." I remember hearing of a pastor who announced one Sunday morning that in the evening service that night he would publicly name the most dangerous member in their church. Needless to say, the church was a packed for that evening worship time. Everyone waited anxiously to hear who this destructive member was, until the pastor directed their attention to James 3:5, reading, "Even so the tongue is a little member, and boasteth great things. Behold, how great a matter a little fire kindleth!" (KJV).

James reminds us that the tongue is a challenging thing to control: "And the tongue is a fire, the very world of iniquity; the tongue is set among our members as that which defiles the entire body, and sets on fire the course of our life, and is set on fire by hell" (James 3:6). David saw this same potential for danger, and sought to govern how he used words, lest he be guilty of bringing harm to others.

"I will guard my mouth with a muzzle." How many times have I wished for a muzzle for my mouth, right after saying something unkind, insensitive, or unnecessary? More than I care to count. David's willingness to be diligent in guarding against misspeaking is a notable and noble precaution. Careless words can do so much harm. We know this, because most of us at some point have been on the receiving end of that hurt or harm. Still, when the opportunity arises we far too often find ourselves speaking before thinking, and once uttered, those words can never be recaptured.

David is looking for the safe ground; he does not want to exacerbate the situation with rash words. This is a valuable lesson for us. Bible teacher Herbert Lockyer wrote, "No lesson is so hard to learn as that of holding our tongue. Yet, David promised that his would be a wise and discreet government of his lips. Socrates reported of one Pambo, an honest, well-meaning man, who came to his friend; desiring to teach him one of David's psalms, he read him this verse. Pambo answered, 'This one verse is enough, if I learn it well.'"

Yet David's desire to guard his speech is not without a down side.

His Emotions

David's silence carries with it a huge emotional price tag. While he guards his tongue, his heart bears the full brunt of his emotions. With his voice David is saying the right things, but his self-restraint in the face of the danger of his circumstances has immobilized him. He is so immobilized, in fact, that he even refrains from doing good. In this situation, David faces the danger warned of centuries later by statesman and author Edmund Burke, who said, "The only thing necessary for the triumph of evil is for good men to do nothing."

This captures a disturbing aspect of the power of fear. When we are threatened, fears cloud our judgment and can impede us from doing the things we know to be good and right. James warns of this when he writes, "Therefore, to one who knows the right thing to do and does not do it, to him it is sin" (4:17). Spurgeon agreed. In his *Treasury of David*, he wrote:

> David was not quite so wise as our translation would make him; if he had resolved to be very guarded in his speech, it would have been altogether commendable; but when he went so far as to condemn himself to entire silence, "even from good," there must have been at least a little sullenness in his soul. In trying to avoid one fault, he fell into another. To use the tongue against God is a sin of commission, but not to use it at all involves an evident sin of omission. Commendable virtues may be followed so eagerly that we may fall into vices.

Wisdom requires balance—a balance that recognizes the value of guarding our tongues while being willing to "speak the truth in love" when necessary.

The Reality of Death

Bob Dylan gave us that memorable cryptic line, "He not busy being born is busy dying."

English playwright and screenwriter Robert Bolt put his own spin on that idea with his words, "Even at our birth, death does but stand aside a little. And every day he looks towards us and muses somewhat to himself whether that day or the next he will draw nigh."

The ancient Greek philosopher Epicurus put in his two cents' worth as well when he said, "It is possible to provide security against other ills, but as far as death is concerned, we men live in a city without walls."

Job would have agreed. Long before any of the above he wisely observed, "Man who is born of woman is of few days and full of trouble" (Job 14:1 NKJV).

Singers, sages, and scholars agree: life is brief, it is not easy, and it always ends in death. In Psalm 39, David faces those same hard realities of life, including the reality of death.

> *My heart was hot within me,*
> *While I was musing the fire burned;*
> *Then I spoke with my tongue:*
> *"Lord, make me to know my end*
> *And what is the extent of my days;*
> *Let me know how transient I am.*
> *Behold, You have made my days as handbreadths,*
> *And my lifetime as nothing in Your sight;*
> *Surely every man at his best is a mere breath."*
> *(Psalm 39:3–5)*

The specter of death hangs over us all like the sword of Damocles. Still, we fight it. We cling to life and breath. Someone has said, "Time is *not* marching on—it's running out!" Few things are as capable of getting our attention as death. It is the elephant in the room that we don't want to talk about, yet can never really avoid. It is all around us all the time, pressing us and pushing us, reminding us that life is all too short.

During my years as a pastor I officiated at dozens of funerals, and one of the things I learned is that funerals do more than force us to deal with the loss of someone we love. Funerals remind us of our own mortality. They force us to acknowledge that one day it will be us lying in that casket.

David faced the reality of death, and he grieved over the shortness of life. Notice the terms he used to try and capture that whisper of brevity.

"Make me know my end, and what is the extent of my days." In the only psalm attributed to him, the great Hebrew leader Moses sang:

As for the days of our life, they contain seventy years,
Or if due to strength, eighty years,
Yet their pride is but labor and sorrow;
For soon it is gone and we fly away. (Psalm 90:10)

That knowledge either leads to fatalism or a sense of personal responsibility. For Moses and for David the choice was to learn to be responsible with how they managed the time they had. Moses affirmed:

So teach us to number our days,
That we may present to You a heart of wisdom. (Psalm 90:12)

And David seems to echo those words. It is the desire to make life count for however long we have it.

"You have made my days as handbreadths, and my lifetime as nothing in Your sight." I don't believe that David is saying that he is disheartened by God's lack of concern for His creatures. I suggest, instead, that he is speaking comparatively—our temporality stands in marked contrast to God's eternality. By comparison, our lives are like nothing.

"Surely every man at his best is a mere breath." Our earthly life is so temporary that it will only stretch as far as the next breath we take. Life truly is as unpredictable and unreliable as that. In the instant of a breath it can be taken away.

A. W. Tozer, in *The Knowledge of the Holy*, eloquently expressed his own lament on the brevity of life: "We poor human creatures are constantly being frustrated by the limitations imposed on us. The days of the years of our lives are short! Life is a short and fevered rehearsal for a concert we cannot stay to give. Just when we appear to have attained some proficiency, we are forced to lay our instruments down."

Life is short. And though we may fight and kick and scream to stretch it further, the fact remains, as David said, "Surely every man at his best is a mere breath." And that is why, like David, we have to make sure that our lives count for something.

The Hope of the Mortal
The November 20, 2006, issue of the *Chicago Tribune* featured a fascinating article on "Understanding Fear of Death." It examined the results of studies done on the fear of death, why most people have it, and why some don't.

> So widespread is fear of death that it is the subject of an academic discipline—the study of death anxiety—producing a substantial amount of literature in the last four decades. Researchers have divided it into various types of fears:

fear of pain, fear of the unknown, fear of non-existence and fear of eternal punishment . . .

Religious faith is no guarantor of peace at the end of life. Nitza Rosario, a chaplain with Rainbow Hospice in Park Ridge, recalled a patient who was a pious woman, but in facing death was terrified. "She was a pillar of her church, but in talking to her, I saw this look of fear in her eyes," Rosario said. "She said, 'There are so many religions; how do you know which is the right one?'"

Faith also can mask fear. One study found that some people who say they believe in an afterlife may actually dread there is none. When college students were hypnotized and asked to rate their fears, they expressed greater fear of non-existence than when they were awake.

One person, when considering the inevitability of death, simply said, "It's coming whether you like it or not. You just have to accept it." Tragically, even those in the family of faith often live lives that seem to say, "This life really *is* all there is."

David does not agree with this fatalistic worldview. He knows all about accumulating wealth you can never ultimately keep, and he describes it. But, he trumpets, that is decidedly not all there is. There is more. There is hope. There is purpose.

Surely every man walks about as a phantom;
Surely they make an uproar for nothing;
He amasses riches and does not know who will gather them.
And now, Lord, for what do I wait?
My hope is in You.
Deliver me from all my transgressions;
Make me not the reproach of the foolish.
I have become mute, I do not open my mouth,
Because it is You who have done it.

Remove Your plague from me;
Because of the opposition of Your hand I am perishing.
With reproofs You chasten a man for iniquity;
You consume as a moth what is precious to him;
Surely every man is a mere breath. (Psalm 39:6–11)

Do you see it? The foolish life of time-bound man is simply not capable of equipping us for eternity. That is why we must be set free from the slavery of time and its limitations—a liberation that only comes as a result of grace.

The Heart Bound by Time

If our mortality consumes us, we see only a life without meaning. David feels like a "phantom" walking around, making an "uproar for nothing" (v.6). The fact is, however, that, as we saw earlier, facing the brevity of life is less crippling than facing a life that seems pointless. The life of a phantom whose existence is a pointless uproar is the dangerous consequence of allowing ourselves to be overwhelmed by our mortality. Only when we move beyond the bondage of time can we live lives of purpose.

In the movie *Pearl Harbor*, American pilot Rafe McCauley travels to England to fly with the Royal Air Force in defense of the embattled island being assaulted by the German aerial blitzkrieg. Upon arriving at the air base, Rafe sees planes that have been shot to pieces and tells his commander that he needs to get in a plane and get in the air right away. The shocked commander asks, "Are all Yanks as anxious as you to get themselves killed, Pilot Officer?" McCauley responds, "Not anxious to die, sir. Just anxious to matter."

The heart bound by time fears pointlessness as much as it does death, and being a meaningless phantom with a pointless uproar is a thought David fears greatly.

The Heart Freed by Grace

Nevertheless, in the midst of it all, David says (v. 7), "My hope is in you"—a sweet, simple affirmation of confidence in the God who brings meaning and purpose to the brevity of life. Only God can overwhelm our sense of futility with His purpose. Only God can defeat our temporary existence with the hope of a life that is everlasting.

It was to that end that Christ came into the world. He came to liberate hearts enslaved by sin (and time's tyranny) with His grace. When standing by the grave of His friend Lazarus, Jesus said to the deceased's grieving sister, "I am the resurrection and the life; he who believes in Me will live even if he dies, and everyone who lives and believes in Me will never die. Do you believe this?" (John 11:25–26).

Martha's response echoed her confidence in the Christ who can conquer the inevitability of death with His own resurrected life, and mirrored the hope that David, in wrestling with his own mortality, affirmed in his God. It is the hope held by the heart set free by grace, the heart that declares:

> *But when this perishable will have put on the imperishable, and this mortal will have put on immortality, then will come about the saying that is written, "*DEATH IS SWALLOWED UP IN VICTORY. O DEATH, WHERE IS YOUR VICTORY? O DEATH, WHERE IS YOUR STING?*" The sting of death is sin, and the power of sin is the law; but thanks be to God, who gives us the victory through our Lord Jesus Christ. (1 Corinthians 15:54–57)*

The Challenge

"Hear my prayer, O LORD, *and give ear to my cry;*

Do not be silent at my tears;
For I am a stranger with You,
A sojourner like all my fathers.
Turn Your gaze away from me, that I may smile again
Before I depart and am no more." (Psalm 39:12–13)

David closes his song of mortality with a prayer that acknowl-edges the reality of life. Hundreds of years after David's journey, the apostle James wrote this spiritually healthy perspective to this same reality:

Come now, you who say, "Today or tomorrow we will go to
such and such a city, and spend a year there and engage in
business and make a profit." Yet you do not know what your
life will be like tomorrow. You are just a vapor that appears for
a little while and then vanishes away. Instead, you ought to
say, "If the Lord wills, we will live and also do this or that."
But as it is, you boast in your arrogance; all such boasting is
evil. Therefore, to one who knows the right thing to do and
does not do it, to him it is sin. (James 4:13–17)

Regardless of medical breakthroughs and technological advances, our lives on this earth are decidedly finite. We can-not by strength of will extend our lives, but we can—and must—extend the influence of our lives. We can regret the limitations that we endure and live accordingly, or we can live our lives to make a difference.

This is a challenge that is not governed by the length of our days, but by the depth of our commitment. Only when we are more concerned with living than we are with dying will we be able to truly live meaningful, victorious, and purpose-ful lives.

Psalm 42

The Heart Broken by Desperation

The mass of men lead lives of quiet desperation.
—HENRY DAVID THOREAU

Nowadays men lead lives of noisy desperation.
—JAMES THURBER

As a "baby boomer," I am part of a generation that has lived its entire life under the shadow of a nuclear mushroom cloud that could come at any moment, creating in people's hearts an engrained sense of helplessness. In my childhood this was best typified by the days of the Cuban Missile Crisis of October 1962. Even as a sixth grader at Highlawn Elementary School, I was painfully aware that if the missiles were launched against the U.S., hiding under our school desks was fairly pointless. As the days of interminable newscasts and dire predictions wore on and on, the pointlessness was replaced by a new emotion for a ten-year-old. Desperation.

A book I had read contributed to that emotional response. It was a science fiction thriller by Pat Frank entitled *Alas, Babylon,* and told the story of a group of people in central Florida. A nuclear exchange had been triggered between the United States and the Soviet Union, the world was plunged into a nuclear winter, and the story followed the attempt of this small band to survive in the face of spreading disease, diminishing food resources, fear of invading armies, and a plethora of other potential disasters. It was a fascinating book, but probably not something a ten-year-old needed in his head while nuclear war was an option being considered by the world's superpowers.

I found myself trying to think of ways to help my family survive the seemingly inevitable holocaust that was looming. I wondered where we could hide, what we could eat, how we could survive. It was a time of crisis for the world, experienced very personally by a little boy in St. Albans, West Virginia.

Although the feared nuclear exchange never occurred, as the years passed the terror and desperation it engendered never fully went away. To some degree, it was simply replaced by others: the assassinations of a president, presidential candidate, and civil rights leader; the war in Vietnam and the concerns about being drafted. Then there were the more localized terrors: my dad being fired from his job with a houseful of kids to feed, chemical plant leaks and scares, and even the comparatively insignificant fear of rejection by the people at school I desperately wanted to accept me. Growing up as a boomer was not easy, but it was educational. It taught me that life is filled with moments, hours, days, months, and sometimes even years of crisis.

As we get older, however, we tend to grow a bit numb to that sense of terror and desperation, and even pretend that we are capable of dealing with it—or so we think.

- We think we have somehow mastered the art of brink-manship.
- We think we can keep our balance as we walk the precarious tightrope of life in a fallen world.
- We think we have escaped the pain or the turmoil or the hurt or the shame.

We think. Then suddenly the crisis intensifies to a level we are not prepared for—like the terror attacks of September

11, 2001—and our carefully constructed house of cards comes crashing down around us and we are no longer so confident. We are no longer so bold. No longer so certain.

In times of crisis, as life begins to overwhelm us, we can, like the writer of Psalm 42, become a desperate soul.

A Desperate Soul

In the movie *Butch Cassidy and the Sundance Kid*, the two outlaws are being pursued by seemingly tireless lawmen ("Who are those guys?") and try every trick they have learned from years of evading the law to escape their pursuers. When they finally run out of tricks, they find themselves perched on a cliff's ledge, looking down at a river of whitewater some 100 feet below and looking up at the gunmen positioning to take them out. The Kid wants to make a stand and shoot it out, but Butch declares that the only hope they have for escape is to jump for the river!

In a hilarious exchange, the Sundance Kid refuses, finally, when pressed by Cassidy, admitting that he can't swim. Laughing uproariously, Butch says, "why, you crazy, the fall will probably kill ya!" With that there is an odd sense of relief, and they jump into the abyss, not sure whether they will swim away or crash on the rocks below. It is one of the more memorable scenes ever filmed and carries a sage reminder—desperate times call for desperate measures.

Desperate times call for desperate measures—or, in the very least, those desperate times sometimes produce desperate people.

Such was the situation of the psalmist as this song begins. (Although David is not named as the author, many Bible scholars believe he wrote this piece, with the intent that it be sung by the sons of Korah.) The psalmist is under siege and can think only of escape. In Psalm 55, the psalmist laments:

I said, "Oh, that I had wings like a dove!
I would fly away and be at rest.
Behold, I would wander far away,
I would lodge in the wilderness." (Psalm 55:6–7)

The desperation of the moment calls for a desperate measure—run away! And In Psalm 42:1 we find an echo of this thought.

A Desperate Flight

As the deer pants for the water brooks,
So my soul pants for You, O God. (Psalm 42:1)

Each year in November in Michigan, where I live, two things are certain. The first is that there will be thousands of deer hunters out in the fields and woods, in tree stands and on the ground. Some hunt for the food, some for the sport, and some to thin the herd.

The second thing that is certain is a consequence of that first thing. The laws of physics tell us that for every action there is an equal and opposite reaction. When hunting season begins, the action is the hunters pouring into the woods, and the reaction is the deer trying to escape. All those deer on the move can make highways a dangerous obstacle course. Believe me, there are few things more terrifying than driving seventy miles an hour on the highway and suddenly seeing a deer dash in front of your car.

For the deer, the fear of pursuit causes the flight mechanism to kick in, and all they can do is run.

Derek Kidner points out that Psalm 42:1, where the deer pants for water, may picture a deer pursued by a hunter—desperate and fearful, overwhelmed by danger. Others, he says, see this more as the imagery of a drought, as we see in Joel 1:20:

> *Even the beasts of the field pant for You;*
> *For the water brooks are dried up*
> *And fire has devoured the pastures of the wilderness.*

This speaks of a slower agony and less hope of deliverance, looking to the provider to supply what tragedy has taken—a provision that may never arrive. In either case, whether pursued by foe or fear, the psalmist is weighed down by the concerns of survival and is fleeing for his life, and the only possible solution is in the God who alone can protect and provide. It is the reality of the life that has been parched by the harshness of life in a desperate world, and the longing for a depth of relief that cannot be found anywhere in that world.

A Desperate Longing

> *My soul thirsts for God, for the living God;*
> *When shall I come and appear before God? (Psalm 42:2)*

Do you see how painful these words are? All of the psalmist's long struggle and spiritual ordeal is encapsulated in the anguished cry of "When?" He longs for God but finds it impossible to discover where or how to connect with the God of hope and find relief in the place of His presence.

Bible student and teacher from years gone by, Matthew Henry, in *Matthew Henry's Concise Commentary*, put it this way: "The psalmist . . . looked upon the living God as his chief good, and had set his heart upon him accordingly; . . . casting anchor thus at first, he rides out the storm. . . . A gracious soul can take little satisfaction in God's courts if it does not meet with God himself there. . . . Living souls never can take up their rest any where short of a living God."

There it is. Eventually, the law of diminishing returns kicks in, and the things we are pursuing are no longer capable of bringing us any joy, hope, or satisfaction. In those moments of clarity, we sense that there must be something higher, something better. Something that can quench our thirst.

David's son, King Solomon, experienced this same struggle. Blessed by God with extraordinary wisdom, Solomon was nonetheless distracted by other things. As the hymn writer put it, Solomon, like us, was "prone to wander, Lord, I feel it, prone to leave the God I love." Solomon describes his journey and his failed attempts to find meaning and purpose in the first two chapters of Ecclesiastes.

Attempt #1: Success

Ruling during Israel's golden age and being sought out by the monarchs of the world for his counsel did not satisfy Solomon's heart. His lofty success seemed pointless, a fact that caused him to use the word *vanity,* which meant "emptiness," to describe it:

> *"Vanity of vanities," says the Preacher,*
> *"Vanity of vanities! All is vanity."*
> *What advantage does man have in all his work*
> *Which he does under the sun? (Ecclesiastes 1:2–3)*

Attempt #2: Wealth and Pleasure

Solomon was the wealthiest man of his day, and even had some 1,000 wives and concubines at his disposal to meet his physical needs. His solemn evaluation of the wealth and pleasure he enjoyed?

I said to myself, "Come now, I will test you with pleasure. So enjoy yourself." And behold, it too was futility. (Ecclesiastes 2:1)

Attempt #3: Escape

Attempting to escape from the harshness of life, Solomon turned to drink. Still, there was no relief.

I explored with my mind how to stimulate my body with wine while my mind was guiding me wisely, and how to take hold of folly, until I could see what good there is for the sons of men to do under heaven the few years of their lives. (Ecclesiastes 2:3)

Attempt #4: Wisdom

The accumulation of knowledge, without purpose for that knowledge, can leave us drowning in a sea of information, as Solomon discovered in the dark shadows of his own frustrations.

Then I said to myself, "As is the fate of the fool, it will also befall me. Why then have I been extremely wise?" So I said to myself, "This too is vanity." For there is no lasting remembrance of the wise man as with the fool, inasmuch as in the coming days all will be forgotten. And how the wise man and the fool alike die! (Ecclesiastes 2:15–16)

Solomon had the resources at his disposal to be completely unhindered in his pursuit of satisfaction, and he tried everything. But, at the end of the day, he concluded his searchings and longings with this tragic statement:

So I hated life, for the work which had been done under the sun was grievous to me; because everything is futility and striving after wind. (Ecclesiastes 2:17)

Solomon discovered what French philosopher Blaise Pascal would describe so eloquently centuries later: that within every human being is a God-shaped void that only God can fill. Or what Augustine spoke of as the restlessness of the human heart that can only be satisfied by God.

In his moment of desperation, it is that God that the psalmist is pursuing. It is that sense of wholeness and fullness that he desires. And nothing else will do!

A Desperate Heartache

My tears have been my food day and night,
While they say to me all day long,
"Where is your God?" (Psalm 42:3)

In the midst of the psalmist's pursuit, however, he must reckon with another factor. As if the fear and desperation were not enough, he feels yet another sting—a sting produced by the barb of ridicule. A sting felt by many at one time or another. Like one young man I know.

It wasn't his fault that he had been born with a learning disability. Although he was very bright, with a sharp mind in matters related to numbers and facts, he struggled with a form of dyslexia. At times, and without warning, the letters and words on a page simply became a jumbled mess that he found impossible to decode. It was frustrating and wearying, but for a kid in school, it was mostly embarrassing. From third grade on, when the condition had been diagnosed, he had been in special classes and had begun making progress. But kids are kids, and soon he began to feel the sting of the comments of other students who began to make fun of him for having to go to the "dumb" classes. That situation only intensified as the years went on, and the boy came home from school heartbroken on a regular basis, confused by the cruelty of his classmates, and even some former friends. Then, when many of the programs for special needs kids began to be canceled due to funding cuts, his parents decided to try home-schooling to reinforce his reading and writing abilities. Still, reading was always a challenge for him—and not a small challenge in a world based on print communication and text.

In his high school years, he re-entered the public school because he wanted to play sports, only to find that the attitudes had gotten no better. If anything, they were worse. The insults and ridicule had grown more sophisticated, carrying an even deeper sting. After a year of insults and verbal abuse, the young man requested that he once again be home-schooled. That was preferable to living daily with such unkindness, despite the potential he had for great success in athletics that had been seen on the soccer field. It just wasn't worth it.

Charles Simmons said that "Ridicule is the first and last argument of fools." He was right.

In Psalm 42 the psalmist describes his "tears"—his own personal heartache and vulnerability as others taunt him and ridicule his faith when God's ways become hard to understand. They see his suffering, and still they hurl verbal abuse, "Where is your God? He isn't there! You are utterly alone and forgotten."

Yet even in his desperation, he sees a faint glimmer of hope. Inwardly, his thirst is for God, and he will not settle for less. He has stated his passion for God (v. 1), then affirmed it (v. 2), and now has paid for it in abuse and ridicule (v. 3). Nevertheless, this stricken deer has chosen the path of the blessed, for he hungers and thirsts for the God of righteousness (Matthew 5:6).

As Kidner wrote, the singer may be a stricken deer, but he is no desert camel, self-sufficient with the deceptive ease of "those who are now full." Real is his fear and pain and struggle, but his eyes once again turn to God for answers. And he will not be disappointed.

A Longing Memory

It was an odd moment—one of those where you are pretty sure you know what someone means, but are still surprised by what they just said. I was at the funeral of a friend, and the pastor was giving the message. In the midst of that message, however, the widow was suddenly overwhelmed by her grief and loss and began to weep, sobbing loudly and uncontrollably. Her adult children reached to hold her and comfort her, but nothing seemed to bring any relief.

At that moment, the pastor, obviously trying to comfort the stricken woman, said, "It's okay. Someday you'll be able to forget." Those words hit the woman like a thunderbolt. The expression on her face made it clear that she had no desire to forget. In fact, forgetting was the last thing she wanted. What she wanted more than anything else was to remember.

The power of memory is an amazing thing. It can remind us of past hurts or of past joys. It can warm our hearts with the thoughts of past experiences, and it can equip us for future trials because of the lessons learned in those experiences. Memory can be destructive or therapeutic, depending on how we use it. Perhaps that is why Alzheimer's disease is so dreaded. We desperately fear the loss of the ability to remember, and all the benefits that remembering can bring to us.

The psalmist, in his season of desperation, pursued and weary, turns to memory for comfort. He remembers, and as he remembers, his bone-weary soul is strengthened.

A Prompting to Prayer

These things I remember, and I pour out my soul within me.
(Psalm 42:4a)

For the psalmist, the heart of the matter is God himself. Rather than trying to solve the matter himself, by faith he turns to the God who loves him, and exposes the full weight of his pain to that Friend.

The fact is that God already knows our pain. He does not need us to bare our souls for Him to know, but God longs for us to "pour out" our souls so that we can see afresh how deeply dependent upon Him we are. And so that we might see again the personal and genuine concern and care our heavenly Father has for His own.

A Procession of Joy

For I used to go along with the throng
and lead them in procession to the house of God,
With the voice of joy and thanksgiving,
a multitude keeping festival. (Psalm 42:4b)

The psalmist then remembers the great celebrations of corporate worship and is reminded that he is not alone in his confident trust. There are others as well—a community of faith—that has embraced the reality of God's presence and comfort and care. His hope begins to be rekindled. He might be by himself, but he is not alone. He might be away from the family of faith, but he is not isolated.

Charles Haddon Spurgeon described the impact of the psalmist's memories well when he wrote in *The Treasury of David*:

When he harped upon his woes his heart melted into water and was poured out upon itself. God hidden, and foes raging, a pair of evils enough to bring down the stoutest heart! Yet why let reflections so gloomy engross us, since the result is of no value: merely to turn the soul on itself, to empty it from itself into itself is useless; how much better to pour out the heart before the Lord! The prisoner's tread wheel might sooner land him in the skies than mere inward questioning raise us nearer to consolation. Painful reflections were awakened by the memory of past joys; he had mingled in the pious throng, their numbers had helped to give him exhilaration and to awaken holy delight, their company had been a charm to him as with them he ascended the hill of Zion. Gently proceeding with holy ease, in comely procession, with frequent strains of song, he and the people of Jehovah had marched in reverent ranks up to the shrine of sacrifice, the dear abode of peace and holiness. Far away from such goodly company the holy man pictures the sacred scene and dwells upon the details of the pious march. The festive noise is in his ears, and the solemn dance before his eyes. Perhaps he alludes to the removal of the ark and to the glorious gatherings of the tribes on that grand national holy day and holiday. How changed his present place!

The psalmist chooses to no longer be consumed by the desperate hour he faces, but rather to be comforted by the God who has accepted his worship in the past, and continues to love and care for him in the present—difficult and painful present though it is.

A Comforting God

One of the reasons I love music so much is the depth of emotion that it carries. Whether it is the awe of Rachmaninoff's Symphony No. 1 in D Minor, or the triumphant crescendo of Handel's "Hallelujah Chorus." Whether it is the pain of loss in Brad Paisley's "I Wish You'd Stay" or the exuberant promise of the Beatles' "All You Need Is Love." The honest anger of Toby Keith's "How Do You Like Me Now?" or the soft loneliness of Michael Bublé's longing to return "Home." Because music resonates with the emotions that are at the very core of our being, it can lift us up and carry us over the roughest roads and the deepest waters.

This was certainly true of the poignant spirituals of early America. While many of them had double meanings, looking both for freedom from slavery as well as the eternal freedom of heaven, the songs acknowledged the care of God in the midst of a savage world experience. Those spirituals lifted people's hearts, as well as their eyes, to the God of heaven and earth. Perhaps nowhere was this expressed more exuberantly than in the spiritual "Swing Low, Sweet Chariot":

Swing low, sweet chariot,
Coming for to carry me home,
Swing low, sweet chariot,
Coming for to carry me home.

I'm sometimes up and sometimes down,
Coming for to carry me home,
But still my soul feels heavenly bound,
Coming for to carry me home.

As they bowed under the cruel yoke of slavery, these men and women sang out their woes and their hopes, encouraging them to look heavenward. Similarly, the psalmist's song, fueled by his powerful memories of shared worship and the God he trusted, has lifted his heart as well. Where once he felt only desperation, now he feels calm. Where once existed panic and pain, now there is peace. In his song, he has been reminded of the greatness of his God and His ability to bring a solution to his struggle, even if that solution is not yet visible.

Needless Despair

Why are you in despair, O my soul?

And why have you become disturbed within me? (Psalm 42:5a)

This is the inner battle we all face. It is a refrain the psalmist repeats in Psalm 42:11 and again in 43:5. The point? We are called to live in eternity with God on our mind, but we also live in time and space with a mind and body that struggle under the pressures of life.

"Why are you in despair, O my soul?" The answer to the question is that he has been in despair because he has become consumed by his burdens instead of having his heart and mind fixed on the God who alone can relieve those burdens.

We also feel the weight of our earthly load and can be consumed by our own desperate hours. As one wise observer has said, "We live in a world that believes its doubts and doubts its beliefs."

Like the psalmist, we need to stop and listen. We need to listen for the voice of the gentle Shepherd who calls to us, "Come to Me, all who are weary and heavy-laden, and I will give you rest" (Matthew 11:28).

What we need in our personal moments of desperation, whether they be quiet or noisy, is to believe our beliefs and doubt our doubts. We need to yield the load to Him and find the rest that only He can give.

Confident Hope

Hope in God, for I shall again praise Him
For the help of His presence. (Psalm 42:5b)

In the midst of his desperation and fear, the psalmist's faith has not been destroyed. In fact, the pressures of life drive him *to* God, not *away* from Him. In a world that seems hopeless, the psalmist returns to the simple reality that only God can offer him true and lasting hope. The question is: Will we allow that same hope to shape our choices and responses to life?

The song writer's confident hope rests in that which is outside him, which highlights two essential truths:

- We are thoroughly inadequate for the things of this life.
- Our God is thoroughly adequate for the things of this life.

These simple truths carry the strength of eternity, and in that strength we rely not on wishful thinking or our own frail humanity, but on meaningful hope in the God who is enough.

Worshipful Trust

For I shall again praise Him
For the help of His presence. (Psalm 42:5b)

The psalmist has made his choice. His desperate circumstances remain unchanged, but his attitude and heart have been changed by the reminder of the help and hope of the Lord.

- He will trust God, even when life is hard and there are no easy answers.
- He will find hope and rest to encourage his weary heart, even when life doesn't make sense.
- He will lean on a strength that is beyond his own strength, even when the watching world says there is nothing there to lean on.
- He will trust God and find rest in Him for his weary, embattled soul.

In his commentary on this psalm, Matthew Henry offers these words of wisdom with practical hope for our day: "See the cure of sorrow. When the soul rests on itself, it sinks; if it catches hold on the power and promise of God, the head is kept above the billows. And what is our support under present woes but this, that we shall have comfort in Him."

These are not empty platitudes. They are the essence of real life in a desperate world. We experience seasons of life where we are pursued, weary, and ridiculed. We face the moments of desperation that either strengthen us or destroy us. The difference is in the choices we make. Will we go it alone, or will we trust Christ for the strength and grace only He can give?

In another generation (1890), Fanny Crosby chose to place her trust in the Savior and expressed that trust in a song that still sings truth to our desperate days as well:

A wonderful Savior is Jesus my Lord,
He taketh my burden away;
He holdeth me up, and I shall not be moved,
He giveth me strength as my day.

He hideth my soul in the cleft of the rock
That shadows a dry, thirsty land;
He hideth my life with the depths of His love,
And covers me there with His hand,
And covers me there with His hand.

Psalm 56

The Heart Broken by Hate

Friends may come and go, but enemies accumulate.
—THOMAS JONES

M y father-in-law, Jim Dickenson, was just a kid when World War II broke out. Growing up in the mountains of rural western Virginia, he had lived the life of a typical kid from the hills, enjoying nothing better than a day with a fishing pole in his hands. With the war, however, he had to grow up quickly. As a teenager, he lied about his age and joined the Army Air Corps, where he was trained as a waist gunner on a bomber and was dispatched to England. But on a mission over Europe, his plane was shot down and he was captured by the enemy. For eighteen long months he was a prisoner-of-war, suffering deprivation, boredom, hopelessness, and mistreatment at the hands of his captors.

Jim was eventually rescued, but he would never be the same. Beaten down by what he suffered during his many months in captivity, he carried deep emotional scars. His wife, Phyllis, a war bride who married him when they had only known each other a month, was unprepared for the impact of the experiences Jim had suffered. Once a carefree youngster with a sunny disposition, he was now prone to deep despair and sudden mood swings, and alcohol became a part of his solution to the problem. He was never an angry drunk, just a very sad and melancholy man whose heart had been imprisoned by man's inhumanity to man.

It was 1975 when I first met Jim. I had begun dating his daughter, Marlene, whom I had met at college. Jim was kind and welcoming, but quiet and reserved—often even detached. He had returned from war in a day long before anyone had heard of "post-traumatic stress disorder" and at a time when people didn't freely talk about the things they felt, and that hadn't changed. It was only years later that I heard of his experiences in the war. It was something that he himself never spoke of, but the abiding influence of the events on his life was unmistakable.

Two surprising things, however, became his way of processing all that he had been through. First, eleven years after he had been liberated from the camp, Jim and Phyllis, unable to have children of their own, decided to adopt. Living in western Virginia, they went to Abingdon in Washington County and adopted a six-month-old baby girl named Kathy. Jim, however, insisted that her name be changed. The surprise? His memory reached back to his time in the camp and one of its few happy memories. Over the camp loudspeaker system his captors would often play the popular music of the day, mostly for the benefit of the guards, and one song resonated with Jim's anguished heart, bringing him a sense of comfort and even peace. The name of that song was "Lili Marlene," so Kathy's name was changed to Lili Marlene. It was surprising to me to hear how out of the darkness of those years could come something of such beauty that he would use that to name his precious baby girl.

Second, whenever we were together, Jim wanted me to join him in watching his favorite movie. Surprisingly, that film was *Stalag 17*, a story of Allied prisoners of war in a Nazi POW camp. He would never talk about what he had experienced, or correlate his experiences to what was happening on the screen, but at certain times Jim would quietly weep over memories triggered by the movie. When the movie ended, he would quietly rise from his seat and leave the room, but it was clear that somehow he felt better. Watching that film was a cathartic experience for him as he remembered his time in the hands of his enemies. A small step of healing for a heart broken by the ravages of war, experienced but never expressed.

A History of Violence

As we turn to Psalm 56, we find that once again David is the psalmist, and this song has an identifiable source. The song's superscription reads: "For the choir director; according to Jonath elem rehokim. A Mikhtam of David, when the Philistines seized him in Gath."

Here, like my father-in-law, David's suffering is the result of his having fallen into the hands of his enemies. His tears flow as the anger of hate-filled men is directed at him.

Some translations render the tune for this song as "The Silent Dove in Distant Lands" or "The Dove on Distant Oaks," perhaps carrying a faint echo of David's lament in the previous song, Psalm 55:6, where he cries, "Oh, that I had wings like a dove! I would fly away and be at rest." He now is that dove and he is fleeing, but he has not found rest. Instead he has found even greater danger—and even deeper hatred.

When did that occur? The story is told in 1 Samuel. David had fled from Saul's murderous intentions, and, of all places, sought sanctuary among the people of Gath—the home of Goliath, the giant warrior David had killed with a sling and a stone in the valley of Elah, establishing his reputation as a folk hero in Israel. He had now gone from the frying pan directly into the fire!

Why would he go to Gath? It seems to be evidence of the sheer desperation that David felt. Once arriving in Gath, however, he received a mixed welcome.

> Then David arose and fled that day from Saul, and went to Achish king of Gath. But the servants of Achish said to him, "Is this not David the king of the land? Did they not sing of this one as they danced, saying: 'Saul has slain his thousands, and David his ten thousands'?"
>
> David took these words to heart, and greatly feared Achish king of Gath. So he disguised his sanity before them, and acted insanely in their hands, and scribbled on the doors of the gate, and let his saliva run down into his beard.
>
> Then Achish said to his servants, "Behold, you see the man behaving as a madman. Why do you bring him to me? Do I lack madmen, that you have brought this one to act the madman in my presence? Shall this one come into my house?"
>
> So David departed from there and escaped to the cave of Adullam. (1 Samuel 21:10–22:1)

What David thought would be a place of refuge had become a place of even greater danger. When the people of Gath reminded the king of David's role in defeating the Philistine armies, once again his great victory became his undoing, for the same song ("Saul has slain his thousands, and David his ten thousands") that had motivated Saul to destroy the young shepherd was now putting him in danger from the people of Gath.

The Ambivalence of a Battered Soul

For three years our family lived in southern California while I attended seminary and pastored a church. Of the many memories we carried out of Long Beach with us, some of the most vivid were of the earthquakes we experienced there. I've encountered very little thus far in my life that is more unnerving than an earthquake. I mean, where do you seek safety when the earth moves and the buildings sway? There is no place to run and no place to hide when terra firma is no longer firm.

I think of that when I read Psalm 56, because I think David's experience in Gath created an emotional earthquake for him.

> *Be gracious to me, O God, for man has trampled upon me;*
> *Fighting all day long he oppresses me.*
> *My foes have trampled upon me all day long,*
> *For they are many who fight proudly against me.*
> *When I am afraid,*
> *I will put my trust in You.*
> *In God, whose word I praise,*
> *In God I have put my trust;*
> *I shall not be afraid.*
> *What can mere man do to me? (Psalm 56:1–4)*

Notice how emotionally fragile David is here. He bounces back and forth from hope in God to fear of his enemies to confidence in God. He is looking for something solid to stand on, yet feels the ground under his feet moving and shaking, and there is no place to run. So, he runs to his God. Still, in ambivalence he bounces back and forth between appeals to God and fear of his enemies.

He begins by appealing to God for grace in the midst of his terror, yet grace is not what occupies his mind. He is fixated on his enemies and the depth of their hatred for him. Notice how in verses 1 and 2 he describes the torment he fears they will unleash on him.

The Actions of His Enemies

Twice David says that his enemies have "trampled" upon him. "Trampled" is an interesting word, and one that appears only a handful of times in the Old Testament. It speaks of crushing, of a thorough destruction, which another translation renders "swallowed up."

His enemies have such hatred for David that they long to utterly destroy him. Little surprise, then, that he also declares that his enemies "oppress" him and "fight" against him.

The Stamina of His Enemies

David twice says that his enemies hammer away at him "all day long," which speaks of their relentless pursuit. It also implies that in his state of mental and emotional weakness and frailty he is incapable of standing up to their continual onslaught.

In J. R. R. Tolkien's *Lord of the Rings: The Two Towers*, three members of the Fellowship of the Ring pursue Orcs that have captured two of their hobbit friends. Day and night they pursue them but never seem to be able to close the distance, causing them to ask, "What evil gives speed to our quarry?" The horror of the evil that these creatures would do is magnified by their seeming ability to inflict torment without need of rest or respite.

David fears a similar fate at the hands of enemies whose pursuit of his destruction seems to never tire or flag.

The Attitudes of His Enemies

But David's enemies do one thing more. Even as they perpetually trample and fight and oppress, they do it "proudly."

"Proudly" is an interesting word choice here. We might expect David to speak of their viciousness or their brutality, but he doesn't. Instead, David is struck by the pride that forms the platform for their actions—a pride that enjoys the suffering it causes and, even more, feels a sense of personal validation at the ability to inflict such torment on another human being.

After I wrote that sentence, I have to admit, it gave me pause. I have had my share of foes over the years, and in those times of conflict experienced great anxiety. Some of that is the product of being a pastor—a reality I didn't fully appreciate until I picked up a book on pastoral ministry and read the chapter entitled "The Pastor as Lightning Rod." That chapter was an epiphany as I realized that something about the nature of leadership causes you to wear a target on your back—whether you know it or not, whether you deserve it or not (and believe me, sometimes you actually *do* deserve it).

Yet I can't say that any of my experiences were as bad as what David is facing. And I don't think he is guilty of hyperbole (after all, this is inspired Scripture). I think the situation was really as bad as he says, and that realization makes me more understanding of the emotional tailspin he is in. This is not lack of faith. It is the reality of a heart experiencing the unrelenting unkindness of hate-filled enemies. That is pretty nasty stuff.

So where can David turn? He is in a kind of no-man's-land, with no place of safety behind or before. And so he turns questioningly to the God who has not yet intervened on his behalf. He is afraid, he is confused, and he is weary. Being the fox is no fun when you find yourself in the middle of a fox hunt.

The Attacks of Those Who Hate

Photography is a powerful medium. There is a reason for the cliché "a picture is worth a thousand words"—so much so that a photograph can linger in your memory for years, perhaps even for the rest of your life. One such photograph shocked me into seeing the cold reality of the civil rights struggles of the 1960s.

When I was a kid growing up in West Virginia, I attended integrated schools and had African American friends at school. Perhaps that is why I was so shocked when I saw the picture of a young black man who, in 1937, had been chained to a tree and tortured with barbed wire and a blow torch. I remember being stunned and horrified by what I was seeing. But mostly I remember being confused. Having been raised in a home that was color-blind, I could not understand the kind of hatred that it took to do such things to another human being. Pictures of the atrocities of the Holocaust affect me the same way, as do pictures of the tribal violence in Africa that results in ethnic cleansing.

Hatred is a viciously ugly thing, and it seems to vent itself only by inflicting pain on those who are unfortunate enough to be the object of that hatred.

David doesn't offer us photographic images of the way his enemies poured out their hatred on him, but his words paint a vivid picture of distress and emotional struggle.

> *All day long they distort my words;*
> *All their thoughts are against me for evil.*
> *They attack, they lurk,*
> *They watch my steps,*
> *As they have waited to take my life.*
> *Because of wickedness, cast them forth,*
> *In anger put down the peoples, O God! (Psalm 56:5–7)*

David is nearly consumed with anxiety for what his enemies intend to do to him. He is not unaccustomed to mindless hate, having received that already from Saul, but this seems to be even more unsettling to him. And once again it will drive him to seek God as his only possible source of relief.

What has David so distraught?

His enemies misrepresent him ("They distort my words"). Words are such valuable currency that we must spend them wisely. Yet even when we are extremely cautious with our words, we find that others can misunderstand them or misuse them. The personal filters that people bring to their listening can interpret our words into meanings that we never intended. And when malicious intent is present, no such misunderstanding is even necessary. All that is required is a willingness to be dishonest at someone else's expense.

His enemies plot against him ("All their thoughts are against me for evil"). There is never a moment when David can relax. Like lions or hyenas, his enemies are constantly circling him, waiting for a flash of weakness they can exploit. They watch, they lurk, plotting against him.

His enemies seek to destroy him ("They have waited to take my life"). No wonder David feels such terror. Not content to distort his words or stalk him or conceive brutalities against him, they want him dead. It is his very life that is at stake.

One wag has said, "Just because you're paranoid doesn't mean they aren't out to get you." For David, however, this is not paranoia. His enemies are real and numerous and powerful— and they *are* out to get him.

David calls upon God to intervene—to angrily destroy those who seek to harm him. He is seeking divine relief from the evils of men.

The Assurance of God's Care

The Merriam-Webster Online Dictionary defines *assurance* as "the state of being assured: as a) security b) a being certain in the mind c) confidence of mind or manner; easy freedom from self-doubt or uncertainty; something that inspires or tends to inspire confidence."

The problem with assurance is that it is essentially an internal thing. Thus a false assurance is possible because assurance can be so easily attached to how we feel about what is happening.

David's assurance, however, was not mere emotion. It was an assurance rooted and grounded in the promises of his God.

> *You have taken account of my wanderings;*
> *Put my tears in Your bottle.*
> *Are they not in Your book?*
> *Then my enemies will turn back in the day when I call;*
> *This I know, that God is for me.*
> *In God, whose word I praise,*
> *In the* LORD, *whose word I praise,*
> *In God I have put my trust, I shall not be afraid.*
> *What can man do to me?*
> *Your vows are binding upon me, O God;*
> *I will render thank offerings to You.*
> *For You have delivered my soul from death,*
> *Indeed my feet from stumbling,*
> *So that I may walk before God*
> *In the light of the living. (Psalm 56:8–13)*

David recognizes that God is aware of the things that are breaking his heart. God has noticed David's "wanderings" as well as his "tears," and both matter to Him.

The thought that God captures the tears of His child and puts them in a bottle, and that He records every tear in His book is amazing. Whether this statement reflects poetic imagery or literal activity by the God of compassion, it is a vivid display of the depth of God's care and concern for our heartaches, whatever their cause.

However, I suspect that if David were like me, he would rather that God prevented his tears than to save them. My human preference would be a life without heartache, without loss or disappointment or grief or unkindness. But as much as I may not understand or appreciate this divine strategy, the reality is that a life without pain is a life without growth. A life without tears is a life that will never fully appreciate joy.

My inclination might be to avoid the heartaches of life, but my heavenly Father is wiser. He knows that apart from trials I will never be all He intends for me to become. Suffering is a necessary—even if unwanted—part of the shaping process that forms us into the likeness of Christ.

"Although He was a Son, He learned obedience from the things which He suffered," says Hebrews 5:8. If Christ had to experience suffering to fulfill the Father's purposes, then why should I not also learn through suffering? What I have to remind myself is that although God does not prevent my tears, neither is He indifferent to the events of my life that can cause those tears.

He is not indifferent to David's struggles either, and it is that assurance that is the key to David's recovery from his despair: "This I know, that God is for me," David boldly declares (v. 9). What confidence in the heart of David—not in the best of times, but in the worst. Not when life is going well, but when it is at its darkest. David is fully assured of God's abiding care for him.

David has now come to the point of such faith in God that he makes no request of God on his own behalf. David's circumstances may still be uncertain; his enemies are still surrounding him. But he affirms that which is certain: God can be trusted. In fact, not only does David refuse to make demands of God, he also reaffirms his own commitment to Him! His commitment takes two great forms: a thankful heart (v. 12) and a faithful life (v. 13).

David, under the duress of enemies who hate him and seek his destruction, declares his willingness to cling to the trustworthiness of God and the dependability of His word. He will give thanks—even without having yet received relief. He will live a life of witness—even in the midst of mistreatment. And he will seek to honor God as he awaits the response of his Rescuer.

Learning to Trust

Charles Weigle is not exactly a household name, but it is a significant one for those who suffer the "slings and arrows" of human hate. Committed to serving Christ, Weigle undertook the difficult and stressful life of a traveling evangelist. Often forced to do without life's basic comforts and to be away from his home and family for long periods of time, Weigle faithfully preached the message of God's love, not knowing how desperately he would personally need that love.

One day he returned home from an evangelistic crusade to find his house empty and his wife and daughter gone. Left behind was a note from his wife calling him a fool and informing him that she'd had enough of the evangelist life.

Alone, abandoned, feeling the pain of rejection, Weigle entered his own personal "dark night of the soul." At times, he even considered suicide. But slowly, painfully, he learned to trust God once again. He eventually reentered ministry and, having found the grace of God's care for his wounded soul, Weigle placed in a song the singular lesson his experience of heartache had taught him. He wrote:

Ev'ry day He comes to me with new assurance,
More and more I understand His words of love;
But I'll never know just why He came to save me,
Till some day I see His blessed face above.

No one ever cared for me like Jesus;
There's no other friend so kind as He;
No one else could take the sin and darkness from me.

O how much He cared for me!

These are words forged in the furnace of a heart broken by unkindnesses and hatred. Just as David learned to turn to his God for comfort when in the hands of his enemies, so Charles Weigle found that God's care was for him a very present help in times of trouble. My father-in-law, Jim, found this same God of comfort later in his own life.

Psalm 56 is a bold reminder of the trustworthiness of the God who loves us regardless of how much people may hate us. And whatever form their hatred takes, we can say with confidence, "O how much He cares for me!"

Psalm 69

The Heart Broken by Stress

*Reality is the leading cause of stress among
those in touch with it.*
—LILY TOMLIN

Charlie Chaplin's classic film *Modern Times* is hilarious,
physical, slapstick comedy, yet it also carries the edginess
reserved for that special kind of humor that hits too close to
home. *Modern Times*, "Chaplin's last 'silent' film, filled with
sound effects, was made when everyone else was making talk-
ies." In it, "Charlie turns against modern society, the machine
age, (The use of sound in films?) and progress. Firstly we see
him frantically trying to keep up with a production line, tight-
ening bolts. He is selected for an experiment with an automatic
feeding machine, but various mishaps lead his boss to believe
he has gone mad, and Charlie is sent to a mental hospital."
Charlie goes through many more escapades before the film
ends. (Quotes from Internet Movie Database, IMDb.com.)

The adventures and misadventures of Chaplin's "every-
man" reveal a deep concern about life in the modern world
and an image of the kind of stress that fosters in the heart of
the harassed and hounded individual the need for escape. In a
sense, Chaplin's message was prophetic. Released in February
of 1936, *Modern Times* can be seen as a clarion warning that life
would soon become so dominated by pressure that the average

person would feel, like Chaplin, that they had lost control, if indeed they ever had it, and that they were being driven—even herded—through life by forces beyond their control.

It is this condition of our own "modern times" that has caused *stress* to become one of the most powerful and commonly used words in the English language. "Everyone is familiar with stress. We experience it in varying forms and degrees every day. In small doses, stress can actually be beneficial to us. It is only when the stress becomes too great, affecting our physical or mental functioning, that it becomes a problem" (www.emedicinehealth.com).

I believe that in many ways Psalm 69 is "a psalm of stress," sung by the psalmist David thousands of years ago, yet with divine relevance for our day. David, however, was not experiencing stress in "small doses." Instead, a tidal wave of mounting pressures threatened to drown him.

The Causes of Stress

Stress is not a force of nature. It does not suddenly appear out of nowhere for no reason. It is a consequence of circumstances, events, relationships, and a variety of other things at work in our lives. In this psalm we discover some of the things that were causing huge stress levels for the singer of this painful song.

Life's Instability

When I was a boy, my father called a family meeting one evening after dinner. It was my first introduction to grownup problems, as Dad explained to us that he had lost his job. He had worked hard and performed well at his responsibilities, but was adamantly unwilling to bend on some of his personal ethical convictions for his somewhat less ethical superiors—and paid the price by having the rug of employment pulled out from under him.

At the time, I was one of five kids (with two more yet to come), and the thought of my dad being unemployed and without income was pretty tough to take. We base so much of our well-being on security and stability, so when the ground starts to give way under our feet we can't find our footing. This happened to David as well.

> *Save me, O God,*
> *For the waters have threatened my life.*
> *I have sunk in deep mire, and there is no foothold;*
> *I have come into deep waters, and a flood overflows me.*
>   *(Psalm 69:1–2)*

Notice that David can't find good ground to stand on; he has no place to regain his stability. The waves of pressure are battering him and he is sinking fast.

Unmet Expectations

Many of us have felt stress as a result of the pressure of expectation—of not ever being "good enough." From childhood, we try to please our parents. In school, we long to be good enough to make the team, terrified that we will be picked last. We want to be part of the popular crowd, with all the status that implies. We want to be good enough, even when we aren't quite certain what "good enough" means. And when we fail to meet those expectations, the disappointment can be crushing.

For David, however, it was not the stress of unmet personal expectations that were the problem. It was the stress of waiting for God to meet his own expectations.

> *I am weary with my crying; my throat is parched;*
> *My eyes fail while I wait for my God. (Psalm 69:3)*

He waits—and waits and waits and waits. But God isn't responding in the ways David had anticipated, leaving his expectations sadly disappointed.

Overwhelming Opposition

Pressure . . . stress . . . when you know that no matter what you do or how hard you try, you simply can't win. The opposition is too overwhelming. This, too, was part of David's experience.

> *Those who hate me without a cause are more than the hairs*
> * of my head;*
> *Those who would destroy me are powerful, being wrongfully*
> * my enemies;*
> *What I did not steal, I then have to restore. (Psalm 69:4)*

David knew what it meant to face overwhelming odds. He'd been doing it all of his life. Bible commentaries agree that there is no "smoking gun" in Psalm 69 that reveals the direct pressure points that David is facing, but they also almost universally agree that the sentiments expressed in this psalm could have been written during any number of David's experiences— when he was hounded by Saul, when he was threatened in the land of the Philistines, when he was driven from his throne by Absalom. Some even speculate that, in his desire to prepare for the building of the temple, David may have been under attack for his motives or his methods in gathering the resources for this massive building project.

What is clear, however, is that he feels badly outnumbered. He says that to number his enemies would be like trying to number the hairs of his head. His powerful, intimidating foes were overwhelming, even for the man who, as a youth, had seen God grant him victory over the giant Philistine, Goliath.

Past victories were of little consolation when present enemies were so numerous.

Personal Failures

Never make important decisions when you are under pressure. That's great advice, but unfortunately, it's often difficult to follow the wisdom of that maxim. Why? Because one of the factors that often contributes to stress is that we *must* make choices at that pressure point, and the ramifications of those choices can last the rest of your life.

Now, David's proverbial chickens have come home to roost. His stress is exacerbated by the fact that it is his own fault that he is in this position. A wrong choice here and there, and the course of his life has been dramatically changed for the worst. It might have begun innocently enough with his decision to stay home from the battlefield, followed by an evening stroll on the roof of his house and a glimpse of a woman bathing. The dangerous choice came, however, when he decided to take a second look, followed by his choice to indulge in a night of forbidden pleasure. Then the unwanted pregnancy, followed by another choice—murder. A series of unwise choices have opened the door for the immeasurable pain of self-inflicted wounds.

While David's sin with Bathsheba may not specifically be in view in this psalm, his words of lament imply that his own wrong decision-making is at the root of his current struggle:

O God, it is You who knows my folly,
And my wrongs are not hidden from You. (Psalm 69:5)

Few things are more painful or more long-lasting than the scarred consequences of self-inflicted wounds. David confesses that, to some degree, the stress he faces is the product of his own failings. To confront the pressures of life is hard enough. Knowing, however, that some of them could have been avoided with better personal choices along the way is a brutal reality.

Public Shame

David is a complex figure. He has been adored and he has been hated. To some he has been a hero, to others a villain. He is "a man after God's own heart" who has committed terrible sins. David has heard the cheers of the crowd and has known the adoration of his people. Now, however, he is despised by the very people who once loved him. And it is especially difficult when public shame attaches itself to someone who is long-accustomed to public acclaim.

> *May those who wait for You not be ashamed through me,*
>   *O Lord God of hosts;*
> *May those who seek You not be dishonored through me,*
>   *O God of Israel,*
> *Because for Your sake I have borne reproach;*
> *Dishonor has covered my face.*
> *I have become estranged from my brothers*
> *And an alien to my mother's sons.*
> *For zeal for Your house has consumed me,*
> *And the reproaches of those who reproach You have fallen on me.*
> *When I wept in my soul with fasting,*
> *It became my reproach.*
> *When I made sackcloth my clothing,*
> *I became a byword to them.*
> *Those who sit in the gate talk about me,*
> *And I am the song of the drunkards. (Psalm 69:6–12)*

Hear his pain in the words he chooses: "ashamed," "dishonored," "reproach," "estranged," alienation, the subject of gossip and disdain. David has reached the zenith of his struggles: he has become an object of disgust.

All of these are stress-inducers and emotionally crippling. David is under back-breaking pressure and has no hope of escape. He is desperately in need of help.

A Cry for Help

Asking for help can be humbling. It requires an acknowledgment of personal inadequacy, which can be a difficult thing to admit. We're more comfortable joining Frank Sinatra in a rousing chorus of "I did it my way" than we are in acknowledging that "I can't make it on my own." Until we come face to face with a situation that we just can't handle. Until we are out of our depth and in great danger. Then we need help, and it costs us something to ask for it. And that is not necessarily a bad thing.

The Basis for His Cry

What causes us to cry for help? What makes us believe that rescue is possible, let alone probable? As the psalmist cries out to God, notice that he is *not* saying, "Help me, God, because I deserve it." He is not claiming any special privilege or position. He does not recite his credentials or past faithfulness as reasons for God's intervention. He simply says, "Help me God, because you are a God of mercy."

> *But as for me, my prayer is to You, O LORD,*
> *   at an acceptable time;*
> *O God, in the greatness of Your lovingkindness,*
> *Answer me with Your saving truth. (Psalm 69:13)*

As he cries for help, David is banking on God's loving-kindness; he believes that God is a God of mercy. And notice that he submits his stress and pressure to God, asking Him to deal with them "in His time."

In his commentary on Psalms, Derek Kidner lifts this idea to the forefront of the request: "the phrase, *At an acceptable time*, controls the request, *answer me*. It is a humble admission that however urgently one may cry out 'make haste' (17), one's times are in God's hand (31:15)."

David is so completely yielded to God's purposes that he is not only willing to seek His help, he is willing to leave the timing of that help to God.

The Nature of His Request

Our prayer lists often more closely resemble a shopping list than a humbling of self before the King of Heaven. David's prayer list is decidedly more straightforward. He prays for one thing and one thing only: rescue.

> *Deliver me from the mire and do not let me sink;*
> *May I be delivered from my foes and from the deep waters.*
> *May the flood of water not overflow me*
> *Nor the deep swallow me up,*
> *Nor the pit shut its mouth on me. (Psalm 69:14–15)*

Some of our most profound prayers are wonderfully brief. We have neither the time nor the inclination to be long-winded. We have only the cry of our hurting heart.

When Jesus' disciples saw Him walking on the waters of the Galilee, Peter asked for permission to join Him on the water. Jesus agreed, and Peter did fine for a few minutes. Then, as Matthew tells us, the reckless water-walker, "seeing the wind, he became frightened, and beginning to sink, he cried out, 'Lord, save me!'" (See Matthew 14:22–30.) Ah, the brevity of desperation.

David's request is also succinct: "Deliver me!" From the mire, and the foes, and the deep waters, and the flood, and the deep, and the pit. "Lord, save me." It is a worthy request to the only One capable of answering it.

The Hope in His Heart

In times of stress, we long for relief, and David cried out for it.

> *Answer me, O LORD, for Your lovingkindness is good;*
> *According to the greatness of Your compassion, turn to me,*
> *And do not hide Your face from Your servant,*
> *For I am in distress; answer me quickly.*
> *Oh draw near to my soul and redeem it;*
> *Ransom me because of my enemies! (Psalm 69:16–18)*

David pleads for quick relief from the stress he faces. His request is still for rescue ("redeem," "ransom"), but behind that request is the need of a heart weary for respite from the pressures and the struggles of a life that quite simply has not turned out as he wished.

The Hatred of Men

This psalm takes a surprising turn as David describes the heartbreak of being alone and encompassed by enemies.

> *You know my reproach and my shame and my dishonor;*
> *All my adversaries are before You.*
> *Reproach has broken my heart and I am so sick.*
> *And I looked for sympathy, but there was none,*
> *And for comforters, but I found none.*
> *They also gave me gall for my food*
> *And for my thirst they gave me vinegar to drink.*
> *   (Psalm 69:19–21)*

His words foreshadow the treatment Christ would receive at the hands of those who hated Him. The bitterness of gall and vinegar mirrors the bitterness of their shameful treatment and cruel hatred (v. 21). All four of the Gospels point to David's anguish as a predictor of Christ's suffering on Calvary, where He was suspended between heaven and earth, yet rejected by both.

The reproach that broke David's heart was the stress that comes upon us when we have no place to turn and feel we have no one to help. No wonder that, in this time of brokenhearted aloneness, David cries to God for help.

A Call for Judgment

While David's experience may foreshadow the experience of Christ, the responses of David and Christ could not have been more different. Christ prayed for the forgiveness of His tormentors, but David prayed for the destruction of his foes.

Sometimes, when under pressure, we find it challenging to perform in a way that is socially acceptable. The stress of the situation tends to strip away the façade and leave us unvarnished—and our responses to the pressure brutally honest. This was certainly true of David in his time of stress.

May their table before them become a snare;
And when they are in peace, may it become a trap.
May their eyes grow dim so that they cannot see,
And make their loins shake continually.
Pour out Your indignation on them,
And may Your burning anger overtake them.
May their camp be desolate;
May none dwell in their tents.
For they have persecuted him whom You Yourself have smitten,
And they tell of the pain of those whom You have wounded.

Add iniquity to their iniquity,
And may they not come into Your righteousness.
May they be blotted out of the book of life
And may they not be recorded with the righteous.
    (Psalm 69:22–28)

David's request for God's judgment falls into the category of the "imprecatory psalms." In an imprecatory psalm, the singer turns his rage on his enemies, calling God to bring down curses and destruction on them.

While I do not necessarily endorse David's rage or his hunger to see his enemies suffer, I believe that we can learn something from the honesty of his prayer. The plainspokenness with which David talks to God indicates a relationship of great confidence. David is willing to trust God with his most intimate emotions, even the ugly ones.

Perhaps it is for such moments of transparent prayer that Paul urged us to consider the intercessory ministry of the Holy Spirit: "In the same way the Spirit also helps our weakness; for we do not know how to pray as we should, but the Spirit Himself intercedes for us with groanings too deep for words; and He who searches the hearts knows what the mind of the Spirit is, because He intercedes for the saints according to the will of God" (Romans 8:26–27). In those moments when we rage with anger against those who harm us, the Spirit of God can intercede on our behalf, "translating" our prayers of vengeance into that which coincides with the purposes of the God we trust. It is to that end that David seeks deliverance from hatred that only the God who one songwriter described as the "lover of our souls" can accomplish.

But I am afflicted and in pain;
May Your salvation, O God, set me securely on high.
    (Psalm 69:29)

Afflicted and in pain. Harsh words to describe a harsh situation. Words of condemnation and judgment. But is that the true heart of David? Or is there more?

A Commitment to Praise

In a time of great duress it is normal to seek an outlet—a release. David's release, however, is a surprising choice. He chooses to find his release by praising God! After such brutal words, this is a bit of a surprise. He has no pity on his enemies, but has nothing but praise for his God. While his emotions may seem confused and clouded in some areas, here his thinking is clear as crystal.

> I will praise the name of God with song
> And magnify Him with thanksgiving.
> And it will please the LORD better than an ox
> Or a young bull with horns and hoofs.
> The humble have seen it and are glad;
> You who seek God, let your heart revive. (Psalm 69:30–32)

Not only does he praise God, he does so by recognizing that God is more interested in the praise of our hearts than in the sacrifices we offer ("an ox or a young bull"). It is something that forms grounds for encouragement. It is a knowledge that begins to untie the knots of stress that have bound him. As one seeking God, he feels his weary heart gaining new life in the praise and worship of the Creator.

The Promise of Prayer

> For the LORD hears the needy
> And does not despise His who are prisoners.
> Let heaven and earth praise Him,
> The seas and everything that moves in them. (Psalm 69:33–34)

Notice that David doesn't *ask* God to hear his prayers. He begins with the presupposition that, in fact, God *does* hear his prayers! This too motivates his praise: after all, he is not forgotten. God hears him in his needy state and cares about the bondage of spirit he has been experiencing ("His who are prisoners").

Liberation and relief, hope and promise, come to him for one, and only one, reason—he knows God is listening.

The Presence of God

For God will save Zion and build the cities of Judah,
That they may dwell there and possess it.
The descendants of His servants will inherit it,
And those who love His name will dwell in it.
(Psalm 69:35–36)

David closes his song with his final consolation: his anticipation of the presence of God and being at home with Him.

Home. There is (or at least should be) no refuge like home for the stressed heart. Sometimes our earthly homes are places of refuge; sometimes they are not. But "home" for David was the promise of God's enduring presence, and the power and comfort that His presence brings. This is the ultimate answer of our heavenly Father for our earthly stress.

In the New Testament, Peter, erstwhile water-walker and one of our fellow-pilgrims in the journey of life, said: "Therefore humble yourselves under the mighty hand of God, that He may exalt you at the proper time, casting all your anxiety on Him, because He cares for you" (1 Peter 5:6–7).

In the midst of our stress, we can, like David and Peter, learn to trust in the God who cares for us, and cast our anxieties on Him.

Is there a heart o'er-bound by sorrow?
Is there a life weighed down by care?
Come to the cross—each burden bearing,
All your anxiety—leave it there.

All your anxiety, all your care,
Bring to the mercy seat—leave it there;
Never a burden He cannot bear,
Never a friend like Jesus.

—EDWARD H. JOY (1871–1949)

Psalm 73

The Heart Broken by Injustice

The true conservative is the man who has a real concern for injustices and takes thought against the day of reckoning.
—FRANKLIN D. ROOSEVELT

Daily on the evening news and in the newspaper we see and read about people suffering and struggling with the hard questions of life.

- A mother weeps outside a courtroom where her daughter's murderer has just been released on a legal technicality. She pleads, "Is there no justice?"
- A father struggles to feed his family by working hard and doing the right thing. But when he thinks of those who are wealthy by illegal means, he wonders, "What's the point of trying to do right? Maybe nice guys do finish last after all."
- A child is rushed to the hospital, the latest victim of a terrorist bomb. His family cries out, "Why him? What did he do to deserve this?"
- A widow sits beside a new grave and sobs, "It's not fair. Why couldn't the drunk driver have been killed instead of my husband? He didn't do anything wrong."

These are only a few of the many questions that haunt those who think about the unfairness, injustice, and inequity of life. What can we say in response to these? Where can we find answers that will restore our confidence not only in justice, but in God?

I think Psalm 73 is a great place to begin our search for justice in an unjust world. Interestingly, this is the third and final psalm in a trilogy of psalms on the Old Testament principle of retribution, which asserted that God blesses the righteous person according to his righteousness, and God judges the wicked person according to his wickedness. This principle is the Old Testament counterpart to the New Testament law of sowing and reaping found in Galatians 6:7–8: "Do not be deceived, God is not mocked; for whatever a man sows, this he will also reap. For the one who sows to his own flesh will from the flesh reap corruption, but the one who sows to the Spirit will from the Spirit reap eternal life."

The principle of retribution was a common assumption among the ancient Jewish people. Because of their limited understanding of the afterlife, the Israelites expected justice to be assured and all accounts to be settled in this life. The problem confronting the psalmist was that this concept of justice didn't always seem to work in the living out of life. The righteous seemed to suffer and the wicked seemed to prosper—and to him that just was not fair! He felt betrayed by life and by God. The lens through which he viewed his suffering was clouded by personal resentment and confusion.

The first psalm in this trilogy is Psalm 34, in which David expresses the basics of the principle of retribution. The second is Psalm 37, in which he approaches a righteous sufferer with this counsel: Trust God and do good. Now, in this final psalm of the trilogy, the psalmist Asaph is the one who is suffering and doubting, and his anguished questions are pointed and personal. What was once objective theological theory or third-person counsel is now personal pain, and the psalmist himself is the one who is struggling for answers.

Hindsight's Wisdom

One of my favorite quotes states, "Life must be lived forward. Unfortunately it can only be understood backward." In other words, sometimes our clearest understanding of life's events comes only when we see those events through life's rearview mirror. Hindsight gives a more meaningful and accurate context to what we have experienced. For example, looking back I can see that the disciplines and challenges of my college years were an important training ground for the twenty years I spent in pastoral ministry, often in ways I never would have imagined. Likewise, as I reflect on the joys and heartaches of pastoral experience, I can now see that God was laying a foundation for what I am doing today. Life often comes into better focus when we view it through the rearview mirror.

Asaph also came to appreciate this view as he looked back on a time of his life that was filled with despair, doubt, and personal pain. He remembered the times he had wondered about the goodness and fairness of God, but now, in retrospect, could make sense of his life. Notice his opening words:

> *Surely God is good to Israel,*
> *To those who are pure in heart! (Psalm 73:1)*

What an opening for a psalm that deals with someone who is questioning the goodness of God in a full-throated way. From the very outset, the psalmist acknowledges that God is good, not only to Israel in general but also to the "pure in heart"—the righteous, those who are totally committed to God.

Remember that the core of his conflict is that the righteous do not *seem* to be blessed. Asaph's heart has been the battleground, where a struggle has raged over whether or not he will trust God with his life. In retrospect, however, he says that he sees that God does bless the pure in heart, but he has learned this lesson the hard way!

> *But as for me, my feet came close to stumbling;*
> *My steps had almost slipped. (Psalm 73:2)*

Again, see the accuracy of the backward glance. Hindsight really is 20-20. The psalmist sees his dangerously wrong attitude that nearly caused him to stumble and reject God. Why did he feel this way? Hear his honesty:

> *For I was envious of the arrogant*
> *As I saw the prosperity of the wicked. (Psalm 73:3)*

Asaph's candor strikes deeply in my own heart. I have to ask myself if I would be so open, so transparent about my own failures. Asaph's painful self-exposure issues a firm challenge to be authentic and honest with myself—and with God.

"I was envious of the boastful," he says, and "I saw the prosperity of the wicked." Asaph was confessing what we often feel but seldom acknowledge: that we are sometimes prone to envy the prosperity of those who do not know God. The psalmist's belief system told him that if he trusted God, everything would turn out right—eventually. But *eventually* seems far away when you are in the midst of suffering and you must watch as others seem to benefit from their wrongdoing. It was the conflict of spirit between what he saw and what he believed.

Life's Inequities

The struggle in Asaph's heart was over the unfairness he saw all around him. Those who had no time for God prospered while people of faith suffered. We see the same today.

A few years ago when I was in Moscow, I was told by Russian friends that poverty there was so deep that teachers were being paid in vodka (to use as barter goods on the streets) and that Moscow's leading surgeon had to grow vegetables in her yard to feed her family. In stark contrast, I heard on a news radio broadcast that Moscow's wealthiest citizen was the owner of the local Mercedes-Benz dealership. This meant that there were still plenty of people in that city who had sufficient resources for luxury automobiles. If highly trained professionals like teachers and physicians were living in poverty, it made me wonder where all the luxury car buyers were getting their money.

Asaph saw apparent injustices too, and what he saw tore at his soul. Describing those who seemed to have the upper hand for all the wrong reasons, he wrote:

For there are no pains in their death,
And their body is fat.
They are not in trouble as other men,
Nor are they plagued like mankind.
Therefore pride is their necklace;
The garment of violence covers them.
Their eye bulges from fatness;
The imaginations of their heart run riot.
They mock and wickedly speak of oppression;
They speak from on high.
They have set their mouth against the heavens,
And their tongue parades through the earth. (Psalm 73:4–9)

This summarizes clearly the conflict between the "prosperity of the wicked" and the "pure in heart." Look at the conduct of the wicked as seen through the eyes of the psalmist:

- **no pains in their death**—they die full and satisfied
- **no troubles or plagues** like other men and women

- **their pride and violence** seem to be rewarded
- **they bulge with abundance**
- **they speak with pride and arrogance**
- **they rob the poor** of the very basics of life
- **they mock God** in all that they do

In addition, it would seem that what particularly troubled Asaph about the prosperous and rebellious was their attitude toward God. They mocked Him in all they did. Notice the conclusions their prosperity led them to declare:

They say, "How does God know?
And is there knowledge with the Most High?" (Psalm 73:11).

Bible commentator Allen Ross writes, "They [the prosperous and rebellious] seem carefree and unconcerned about tomorrow. For them life is now, and now seems to be forever." Why? Because they felt protected from the normal pains of life (vv. 4–6), so they assumed they were also invulnerable to any divine response to their attitude, sin, and mockery.

Behold, these are the wicked;
And always at ease, they have increased in wealth. (Psalm 73:12)

Despite their evil behavior, they seem to prosper. No wonder Asaph is frustrated. This apparent unfairness had fueled his confession in verse 3: "I was envious of the arrogant as I saw the prosperity of the wicked." It's not hard to imagine that in similar circumstances we too would cry out, "It just isn't fair!"

But Asaph's frustration with life's apparent inequities was just the beginning. How he responded to these injustices was a greater problem.

Frustration's Response

Faith Hill, the well-known country music artist, sings a song called "When the Lights Go Down." It's a song of pain, loneliness, and, most of all, honesty. It describes an alcoholic bartender wrestling with his desire for another drink, a former Hollywood star who has been abandoned by her "friends" after her fame fades, and a person struggling with the realities of a broken relationship and the regrets it has produced. It is a song about the realities of life and the hard questions generated by those realities. The chorus speaks of the emptiness of life ("when you feel that hole inside your soul") and its seeming lack of purpose and worth—an emptiness that becomes inescapable "When the lights go down and there's nothing left to be."

These words, I think, could also describe Asaph's sense of disillusionment. There are few verses in the Psalms where gut-level, honest, human emotion is more clearly seen than in verse 13:

> *Surely in vain I have kept my heart pure*
> *And washed my hands in innocence.*

"In vain" captures the same note of despair heard in Solomon's book of Ecclesiastes. When he cried, "All is vanity," he was saying that life had no worth or value, that all he had attempted had been worthless. He no longer valued purity and righteousness. He was ready to give up and sell out.

Yet at the heart of this is a hard truth to hear. For the reality is that for Asaph (or any of us) to decide that life is all in vain is tragically self-centered. What he really appears to be saying is: "What do I get out of it? . . . When does my back get scratched? . . . What's in it for me?"

In the film *Field of Dreams*, Ray Kinsella builds a baseball diamond in the middle of his cornfield and miraculous things happen—but only for other people. Finally, in exasperation, he declares, "I have done everything that I've been asked to do! I didn't understand it, but I've done it; and I haven't once asked, 'What's in it for me?'" When his friend Joe asks, "What are you saying, Ray?" Kinsella responds, "I'm saying . . . what's in it for me?"

That sounds a lot like Asaph's thinking. A tremendous weight of resentful anger was lodged behind the words of verse 13. And beyond that, Asaph had become so disillusioned that he felt being pure in heart just didn't seem to be worth it. After all, what did he get for his spiritual commitment? Nothing but trouble and chastening.

> *For I have been stricken all day long*
> *And chastened every morning. (Psalm 73:14)*

When it seems as if God is not in control, our doubts can make us want to give up. Purity of heart and life just don't seem to be worth it.

Asaph's response is very human: "It doesn't make sense— why bother?" So what does he do? Surprisingly, he pauses.

> *If I had said, "I will speak thus,"*
> *Behold, I would have betrayed the generation of Your children.*
> *(Psalm 73:15)*

He wants to declare ("thus" refers to verses 13–14) his disapproval of God's handling of life, but he stops short. Why? It is not because of spiritual awakening; it is because of his sense of moral responsibility. He resists expressing all that is in his heart because he realizes that it could cause great hurt and disillusionment among the younger generation.

This is so critical, for it is here that the wisdom of the righteous starts to take back the heart that almost slipped (v. 2). This is Asaph taking his first step back from the edge of the abyss, pulled back by his sense of moral responsibility.

To understand this more fully, we must understand that Asaph was in a position of leadership. He was David's chief musician (ancient Israel's equivalent of a Music and Worship Leader), as well as being a songwriter and a prophet (1 Chronicles 16:5; 25:2; 2 Chronicles 29:30). Such a position carried with it great responsibility because of its influence. But along with the privilege of such a position went the burden of how that position was used to impact people's lives.

Asaph was a man of spiritual influence who was beginning to doubt the goodness of the God he led people to worship. He wanted to abandon all he had been committed to. But he looked ahead and saw the negative impact such a choice would have on those around him. Like a stone tossed into a smooth lake, the rippling effect of his failure would move outward and affect those far beyond his immediate circle.

All shortsightedness and spiritual failure is dangerous. But the potential harm is compounded by the magnitude of a person's scope of influence.

So where does that leave our troubled friend?

When I pondered to understand this,
It was troublesome in my sight. (Psalm 73:16)

He suffers. And what intensity of suffering it is! Even his attempt to comprehend it all fills him with agony!

When will there be answers for the questions?
When will there be relief from the suffering?
When will there be justice in the world?
When will it all make sense?

Wisdom's Answers

One of the most enduring TV home-repair programs, *This Old House*, recently added a new segment called "Ask *This Old House*." People are encouraged to write or email their questions to the program's experts about plumbing, gardening, carpentry, or any other projects. The answers or solutions are then demonstrated on the show. My wife and I spent years involved in the process of renovating our own "old house," so this is the kind of help that is of special interest to us.

But there are other questions that can't be answered by the media and its army of experts. Sometimes we don't find the answers we need until we find ourselves in the presence of God himself. This was Asaph's experience as he continued to struggle:

> *Until I came into the sanctuary of God;*
> *Then I perceived their end. (Psalm 73:17)*

The agonizing cry of the hunchback of Notre Dame, "Sanctuary, sanctuary!" becomes the cry of all those who are suffering. Quasimodo saw the sanctuary as a place of refuge and protection. Asaph, however, discovered it to be the place where he could find answers.

The word *sanctuary* appears throughout the Old Testament. Sometimes it is used to speak of the tabernacle, the tent of meeting that was the place of worship for Israel prior to the building of the temple in Jerusalem (Exodus 25:8; 36:1, 6). Other times it appears to refer to the temple itself (1 Kings 6).

Sometimes, however, *sanctuary* doesn't refer to a physical location but to an idea—the idea of abiding in the presence of God (Isaiah 8:14). It is what David longed for in Psalm 23 when he anticipated "still waters" where the Lord, his Shepherd, would restore his soul. It's what Christ himself sought when

He frequently moved away from the crowds, the work, and the disciples and went to spend time alone with His Father. *Sanctuary* suggests the idea of a place set apart for spiritual protection, rest, and renewal. Every one of us needs such a place—a spiritual hiding place where our hearts are restored and strengthened for the struggles of today and the challenges of tomorrow.

Now, at last, Asaph begins to see the truth beyond the circumstances. In verse 17, we find him "in the sanctuary"—the place of worship—and that ushers him into a new perspective. He has been beset by the onslaught of the temporal, but now gets a point-of-view that is laced up by the eternal. In the presence of the holy God, the inequities of life and the apparent prosperity of the wicked are overshadowed by a new set of insights. His relationship with God brings fresh light to his struggling despair and darkness.

"The solution begins when the psalmist turns to God," writes Derek Kidner, "not as an object of speculation, but as an object of worship."

Asaph sees . . .

The End of the Wicked

Then I perceived their end.
Surely You set them in slippery places;
You cast them down to destruction.
How they are destroyed in a moment!
They are utterly swept away by sudden terrors!
Like a dream when one awakes,
O Lord, when aroused, You will despise their form.
    (Psalm 73:17b–20)

"Their end" refers to the alleged "prosperous wicked." Only in the perfect wisdom of God can this be reconciled, but retribution will prevail. They will bear the judgment of God, fully and completely, and it is a judgment from which there is no escape.

This is not cause for celebration for the psalmist, but it is cause for awakening. At last he can take the long view and can rest in the truth that justice will have its day.

The Beginning of Wisdom

When my heart was embittered
And I was pierced within,
Then I was senseless and ignorant;
I was like a beast before You. (Psalm 73:21–22)

Asaph recognizes his condition as foolish. Why? Because his focus has been on acts of injustice instead of on the God who *is* justice. To allow such conflict of faith to overwhelm us is to set aside the comfort and peace that faith is intended and designed to bring.

Now, however, the psalmist's renewed perspective is coming clearly into focus.

- He sees what he almost did *to himself* (v. 2).
- He sees what he almost did *to the brothers* (v. 15).
- He sees his attitude and actions as an affront and an offense to *the God who is perfectly just* (vv. 21–22).

Asaph had to learn the hard lesson that God is to be trusted, even when life doesn't make sense. That God remains in control, even when life feels out of control.

The Instruction of God

Nevertheless I am continually with You;
You have taken hold of my right hand.
With Your counsel You will guide me,

And afterward receive me to glory. (Psalm 73:23–24)

Asaph learns that as he trusts God, the benefits he receives can carry him through the moments and episodes of doubt and despair. God will be with him, uphold him, guide him with His counsel, and receive him into glory.

Does that sound like the treatment of a God who has forgotten and abandoned us? Never. It sounds like the treatment of a God who never leaves us nor forsakes us, never abandons us, and always sticks closer than a brother to us. He never forgets us. On the contrary, His care is ever complete as He ministers in grace to His child.

What Asaph Learned

In the closing verses of Psalm 73, Asaph recounts what he has learned from his struggle. As we examine these concluding thoughts, we see four profound principles emerge that can be applied to life under any circumstances.

Principle 1: God is my resource.

Whom have I in heaven but You?
And besides You, I desire nothing on earth. (Psalm 73:25)

Asaph realized that, ultimately, God was all he had or needed. He could rest in God's care and have the confidence that nothing else could be compared to his Lord.

Principle 2: God is my strength.

My flesh and my heart may fail;
But God is the strength of my heart and my portion forever.
(Psalm 73:26)

For those moments when Asaph was tempted to rely on his own strength or to produce his own solutions, he had discovered that only in God could he find the unending strength he needed both now and forever.

Principle 3: God is responsible for justice.

For, behold, those who are far from You will perish;
You have destroyed all those who are unfaithful to You.
(Psalm 73:27)

Asaph had envied the godless and their prosperity (v. 3). He had struggled with the apparent inequities of life (vv. 4–12). He even came to the point of feeling that he had lived for God in vain (v. 13). But in the end Asaph acknowledged that those matters must be entrusted to God. As Abraham said, "Shall not the Judge of all the earth deal justly?" (Genesis 18:25). Yes, and Asaph had learned to trust that the Lord, in His own timing and wisdom, would deal mercifully but justly with all the inequities of life.

Principle 4: I am responsible for my nearness to God.

But as for me, the nearness of God is my good;
I have made the Lord God my refuge,
That I may tell of all Your works. (Psalm 73:28)

Asaph's responsibility was not to pass judgment on the world or try to manipulate justice out of injustice. Like James, Asaph learned that his responsibility in all of life was to "Draw near to God and He will draw near to you" (James 4:8).

So, what was Asaph's conclusion? It was the confident assurance that even when life seems unfair, God will always be fair. By faith, Asaph finally understood and believed—and he ended up with a deep, tested, personal conviction of the confession he alluded to as he began his story: "Surely God is good to Israel, to those who are pure in heart" (v. 1).

At the end of his season of struggle with doubt, he realized that God does bless the "pure in heart." Which is why Christ himself could declare: "Blessed are the pure in heart, for they shall see God" (Matthew 5:8).

The Difference Perspective Makes

The Bible doesn't promise that those who follow Christ will have a life free of pain, difficulty, or injustice. Christians are not exempt from struggle, heartache, or disappointment. Therefore, we sometimes find that in the midst of periods of joy and blessing will come episodes when we desperately need a renewed perspective.

The Bible promises that those who believe in Christ will have a Companion on the journey to help, encourage, and strengthen them in whatever may come their way. He is the One who has promised: "'I will never desert you, nor will I ever forsake you,' so that we confidently say, 'The Lord is my helper, I will not be afraid. What will man do to me?'" (Hebrews 13:5-6).

He is our sanctuary. To be able to have this confidence is to live a life that is an exclamation point in a world of question marks. This was the hope that allowed Fanny Crosby, though stricken by blindness, to write songs of joy, peace, and heaven. Maybe this is why, among the hundreds of hymns she wrote, some of her best lyrics are found in this hymn:

> *All the way my Savior leads me*
> *What have I to ask beside?*
> *Can I doubt His tender mercy,*
> *Who through life has been my Guide?*
> *Heav'nly peace, divinest comfort,*

Here by faith in Him to dwell!
For I know whate'er befall me,
Jesus doeth all things well.
For I know whate'er befall me,
Jesus doeth all things well.

What great words! Not from a person who had a painless life of ease and comfort, but from a woman who had learned that regardless of the circumstances and struggles of life, our Lord does all things well. Knowing God and trusting His goodness keeps us from seeing only our external circumstances and wrongly assuming that God is not in control, or is not fair, or does not care.

This difference in perspective comes from knowing God deeply. Only then can we trust Him completely. In the sanctuary, Asaph learned that this kind of relationship is founded and fostered in worship. It interjects the eternal into the daily issues of life. And it reminds us that God doesn't settle His accounts on our schedule.

Psalm 22

The Heart Broken by Sin

*For the wages of sin is death, but the free gift of God
is eternal life in Christ Jesus our Lord.*
—THE APOSTLE PAUL, ROMANS 6:23

I saac Watts was the son of a congregational minister who
followed his father into pastoral service. In 1707, while
serving as the minister of Mark Lane Chapel in London, he
penned poetic words that would later become one of the great
and timeless hymns of the faith, "When I Survey the Wondrous Cross." In a day when most hymns drew their lyrics from
biblical texts, Watts was creative. Wanting to prompt a more
personal worship experience, he crafted a communion hymn
that focused on the believer's perspective of the cross of Christ,
and the devotion that cross should inspire. The website Selah
(www.selahpub.com) says this of the great hymn:

> One of the first English-language hymns to use the word
> "I" and to focus directly on personal religious experi-
> ence, "When I Survey" holds an important place in the
> history of hymnody. It offers an example of how Watts,
> sometimes called the father of English hymnody, enlarged
> the boundaries of English sacred song beyond the metri-
> cal psalms to include freer verse that readily lent itself to
> new musical settings.

"When I Survey" is a graceful hymn, elegant and reverent, and it forces us to consider the extraordinary impact of our sin and its penalty on the Son of God. Long before Isaac Watts, however, and even long before the cross, the hymnal of the Bible—the book of Psalms—offered a psalm that surveys the wondrous cross.

Psalm 22 is sobering, heart-wrenching, painful, and glorious. It is David's inspired prophecy of the cross of Jesus Christ hundreds of years before crucifixion was even invented. This song is a staggering monument to God's eternal plan of redemption. Of Psalm 22, Martin Luther wrote:

> This is a kind of gem among the psalms, and is peculiarly excellent and remarkable. It contains those deep, sublime, and heavy sufferings of Christ when agonizing in the midst of the terror and pangs of divine wrath and death which surpass all human thought and comprehension. I know not whether any psalm throughout the whole book contains matter so weighty, or from which the hearts of the godly can so truly perceive those sighs and groans, inexpressible by man, which their Lord and Head Jesus Christ uttered when conflicting for us in the midst of death, and in the midst of the pains and terrors of hell. Wherefore this psalm ought to be most highly prized by all who have any acquaintance with temptations of faith and spiritual conflicts. (Cited by Herbert Lockyer in *Psalms*.)

And that is why I have chosen to consider this psalm last. We have looked deeply into the heartache that comes from living in a fallen world. We have seen the impact of sin and evil and human frailty on the lives of people weak and strong, young and old. But for all the heartache that our sin causes to us and to others, that cannot compare to the way that our sin broke the heart of the Savior.

Psalm 22 is a powerful song of suffering, death, and sin-bearing in which David steps into the sandals of the coming Redeemer. Here we see the cross from the perspective of the heart of Christ. Here we see the heart of God broken by the awful penalty of human sin.

The Cry of Abandonment

She was crushed. This wasn't the way she had planned her life; it wasn't even remotely close to what she had anticipated, but that didn't change the reality. Through sobbing tears, she shared with me that her husband had left her and their children, and had taken up with another woman. Her jumbled sense of embarrassment, loss, rejection, and anger were painfully etched on her face as she talked through her broken marriage and broken dreams. She had been abandoned, and few heartaches in life cause more personal anguish.

Abandonment was a significant part of the suffering of Christ on the cross as well; and the Savior cried out the opening words of David's psalm as He endured the horrors of the crucifixion: "My God, my God, why have You forsaken me?"

My God, my God, why have You forsaken me?
Far from my deliverance are the words of my groaning.
O my God, I cry by day, but You do not answer;
And by night, but I have no rest. (Psalm 22:1–2)

In this abandonment, as He suffered the rejection of the Father to atone for our sins, our Savior endured the deepest pain of His entire passion. To quote James Stalker in *The Trial and Death of Jesus Christ*:

How near He is to us! Never perhaps in His whole life did He so completely identify Himself with His poor brethren of mankind. For here He comes down to stand by our side not only when we have to encounter pain and misfortune, bereavement and death, but when we are enduring that pain that is beyond all pains, that horror in whose presence the brain reels, and faith and love, the eyes of life, are put out—the horror of a universe without God, a universe which is one hideous, tumbling, crashing mass of confusion, with no reason to guide and no love to sustain it.

As He absorbs in himself the sins of the world, Christ bears our curse, and, as a result, our separation from God caused by our sin. Pastor H. C. Leupold wrote:

It must be noted that the "why" is not so much an attempt to find the deepest reason of it all as it is a complaint as to the incomprehensibility of it all. Surely, God had forsaken Him who utters this complaint, but the reason was that He had made Him to be sin that knew no sin (2 Cor. 5:21). No man can fathom the mystery of this outcry and what it meant in the experience of Christ. But of this we can be assured: the God-forsakenness was real.

Yet, as terrible as this sense of abandonment was, what brought His anguish to its fullness was that all the suffering Jesus was enduring was from the very hand of His Father himself! As stated in Isaiah's prophecy, He was being "smitten of God," for "the Lord was pleased to crush Him" (Isaiah 53:4, 10). David refers to this later in the psalm when he declares:

My strength is dried up like a potsherd,
And my tongue cleaves to my jaws;
And You lay me in the dust of death. (Psalm 22:15)

Christ is not just facing death as His *Father* lays Him "in the dust of death." As Robert Alden wrote in his commentary on the Psalms:

> Note that it is God, not the enemy, who has brought the sufferer to death. He acknowledges God's sovereignty. Still He sees Himself as part of the divine plan for the ages. Though dogs and evildoers nail His hands and feet, though soldiers crucify Him at the command of the government and at the urging of the madding throng incited by the Jewish leaders, yet it is God His Father that brings Him to the death (v. 15). That is the key verse in this psalm; it is one of the essential doctrines of the Christian faith. God willed that Christ should die.

It was that consciousness of His God-forsakenness and the realization that God himself was the source of the suffering that, in His sin-bearing sacrifice, brought our Lord His deepest pain. But there also were other elements of the suffering of the Lamb of God.

The Cry of Aloneness

If the abandonment of Christ by the Father was reflective of the spiritual suffering of Christ in His crucifixion, His rejection by the people He had come to redeem speaks to His emotional suffering. One person described Christ as, "Suspended between heaven and earth—and rejected by both." John 1:11 agrees, as John sadly states of Christ, "He came to His own, and those who were His own did not receive Him." David also had predicted this element of Christ's sufferings:

> *But I am a worm and not a man,*
> *A reproach of men and despised by the people.*

All who see me sneer at me;
They separate with the lip, they wag the head, saying,
"Commit yourself to the LORD; let Him deliver him;
Let Him rescue him, because He delights in him. (Psalm 22:6–8)

What makes this so shocking is its contrast to how Christ had been received for much of His public ministry. Called "Son of David" and considered the Messiah by many, He had been triumphantly welcomed into Jerusalem aloft the praise of the crowds. Only a few days later, however, Christ endured abuse and rejection from those who stood by and watched the events of Calvary. A description of the crowd at the cross is found in the next verses of this psalm, forming a vivid parallel to the Gospel accounts of the passion of the divine Sufferer.

Their Appearance

These who mock and abuse the Savior are described in harsh terms. From God's perspective, they are not seen as men at all, but as wild animals!

Many bulls have surrounded me;
Strong bulls of Bashan have encircled me.
They open wide their mouth at me,
As a ravening and a roaring lion . . .
For dogs have surrounded me;
A band of evildoers has encompassed me. (Psalm 22:12–13, 16a)

The intent of this passage is not so much a literal description of the scene at Calvary as a figurative portrait of sinful men from the divine perspective. The scene is similar to two different descriptions of the kingdoms of men in Daniel. In Daniel 2, these kingdoms are viewed by men and seen as precious metals, but in Daniel 7 those same kingdoms are seen by God as raging beasts. Such is the view here, as the psalmist speaks in strong and very descriptive terms:

- "strong bulls"—This is a picture of the common cattle of the Galilean region; cattle which were vicious toward approaching people and generally destructive.
- "a roaring lion"—Charles Haddon Spurgeon said, "Like roaring lions they howled out their prey, and longed to tear the Savior in pieces, as wild beasts raven over their prey."
- "dogs"—This is a description of the scavenger animals of the first century. The rats of that generation, these dogs were dangerous, diseased, and destructive.

Their Actions

Not content to pour insults on the Christ, these beastlike men acted out their disdain for Him as well:

They divide my garments among them,
And for my clothing they cast lots. (Psalm 22:18)

Here we see one of the most prophetic statements in this psalm of suffering. John Stevenson, a gifted preacher from the mid–nineteenth century, wrote this about the dividing of Christ's garments: "Trifling as this act of casting the lot for our Lord's vesture may appear, it is most significant. It contains a double lesson. It teaches us how greatly that seamless shirt was valued, and how little he had to whom it belonged. It seemed to say, this garment is more valuable than its owner . . . How cheaply Christ was held!"

Their Attitude

Tragically, however, the words and actions of the crowd were merely the venting of the ugliness that was in their hearts.

Commentator Derek Kidner says their attitude was rooted in hatred for several reasons, including resentment, the compulsion of mob mentality, greed, and perverted tastes. They enjoyed the "harrowing spectacle simply because sin is murderous, and sinners have hatred in them."

Perhaps, however, it is the phrase "they look, they stare at me" that so clearly reveals the wickedness of men's hearts. "He was reduced to a state of misery that should have produced some pity in the hearts of onlookers. Instead they 'gaze' heartlessly with some measure of satisfaction. They may even be said to 'feast their eyes on him'" (H. C. Leupold).

All of these details of the sufferings of Christ, as He was rejected by the very men and women He had come to redeem, are fully and minutely fulfilled in the crowd at the foot of the cross, multiplying the Savior's suffering. The appearance, actions, and attitude of the crowd at the cross—like wild animals dividing His clothing because they can't tear into Him, then staring with pleasure at the horrors of the crucifixion of the Son of God—show mankind at its very worst. Yet it simultaneously shows grace at its fullest and purest because it was for that very crowd that the willing Sacrifice was suffering alone, abandoned by the Father and rejected by the crowd.

The Cry of Anguish

The film *The Passion of the Christ* graphically portrayed the brutality of death on a cross in all its bloody horror. The controversial film generated extensive media coverage, but perhaps the most interesting clips that were run on newscasts were of people exiting theaters with eyes red and cheeks tearstained. The ugly reality of what crucifixion meant in terms of physical suffering was new to many, and it impacted them greatly.

In Psalm 22:14–16, David turns his attention to physical suffering that offers an image of the physical suffering of Christ on the cross.

> *I am poured out like water,*
> *And all my bones are out of joint;*
> *My heart is like wax;*
> *It is melted within me.*
> *My strength is dried up like a potsherd,*
> *And my tongue cleaves to my jaws;*
> *And you lay me in the dust of death.*
> *For dogs have surrounded me;*
> *A band of evildoers has encompassed me;*
> *They pierced my hands and my feet.*

Crucifixion was the cruelest of deaths because of the horrific pain it inflicted on the condemned. In David's prophetic anthem, four key phrases turn our minds to the dreadful nature of that physical pain.

- "I am poured out like water"—This refers to the physical dehydration that resulted from being crucified, as if the very strength and life was being wrung from Him like water from a washcloth.
- "All my bones are out of joint"—This refers to the stretching of the body on the cross and then the sudden shock as the cross was dropped into the ground, causing the joints of the shoulders and elbows to tear and separate, producing excruciating pain.
- "My heart is like wax"—Some see this as a metaphor for a loss of courage, but I think it may refer to the physical phenomenon of the rupturing of the heart described in John 19:34, when one of the Roman soldiers pierced the

side of Christ with his spear to reveal blood mingling with water in the chest cavity—a by-product of a truly broken heart.

- "They pierced my hands and my feet"—The literal fulfillment of this statement in crucifixion is obvious, and is probably the one statement in the psalm that most plainly points to death on a cross. The nails that penetrated the hands (or wrists) and feet attached the sufferer to the instrument of his execution to assure that there would be no escape from the death penalty.

The amazing clarity of these terms as they relate to the cross is all the more remarkable because crucifixion was not known in David's time. That torturous method of execution would not be used for several hundred years, long after David, but long before the death of Christ.

Spiritual suffering. Emotional suffering. Physical suffering. As outlined by David's song, they may appear to have happened in some consecutive fashion. Yet, in reality, the Lord Jesus Christ experienced all of these layers of suffering simultaneously, piling one upon the other:

The abandonment of the Father was compounded by . . .
The rejection of the people was amplified by . . .
The untold suffering of death by crucifixion.

The hateful hearts of sinful men found full vent in those awful moments on Calvary. Of these men, Robert Alden wrote, "For years they had surrounded Christ, waiting for the opportunity to gore Him. As a hungry salivating lion, they lurked in secret to take Him. And now, they have Him on the Cross—dehydrated and hungry, seemingly helpless" (*Psalms, Volume 1: Songs of Devotion*).

The Cry of Acceptance

The amazing thing about all these levels of anguish is that they could not have happened had the Son of God, the willing sacrifice, not allowed it. Jesus said, "No man takes my life from me. I lay it down willingly!" (John 10:18, my paraphrase). In the words of Christ we hear His willingness to endure all these things.

Why? Because of the powerful results that God the Father would accomplish through them! Notice the reach of the cross and its work:

- To the Jews—"From You comes my praise in the great assembly." (v. 25)
- To the Gentiles—"All the ends of the earth will remember and turn to the Lord, and all the families of the nations will worship before You." (v. 27)

This is the psalmist's version of Romans 1:16: "For I am not ashamed of the gospel, for it is the power of God for salvation to everyone who believes, to the Jew first and also to the Greek [the Gentile]." The Lord Jesus Christ, our willing substitutionary sacrifice, accomplished all of this!

They will come and will declare His righteousness
To a people who will be born, that He has performed it.
(Psalm 22:31)

"He has performed it." What a statement of victory! Derek Kidner declares, "The psalm that began with a cry of dereliction ends with the word 'He has wrought it,' an announcement not far removed from our Lord's great cry, 'It is finished.'"

The writer of the book of Hebrews had it right: "fixing our eyes on Jesus, the author and perfecter of faith, who for the joy set before Him endured the cross, despising the shame, and has sat down at the right hand of the throne of God" (Hebrews 12:2). What was that joy? The joy of the powerful results brought about by His great suffering.

F. B. Meyer, the great British minister and expositor of the mid-1800s, put it this way in *Gems from the Psalms*: "There is surely here a forecast of the effects of the death of the Cross, first on the Jews (v. 23), but also in these verses (vv. 27–31) on the Gentiles. The ends of the earth converted, the usurper dethroned (v. 28), the resurrection accomplished (v. 29), and the seething of a spiritual seed to satisfy the travail of the Redeemer's soul!"

This is why Jesus willingly sacrificed himself ("no man takes my life"). This is why He accepted the sufferings that we deserved, that He might bring to himself, and to the Father, a redeemed people from all the nations of the world—cleansed, forgiven, and glorified forever.

The Darkness and the Glory
Of Psalm 22, Charles Haddon Spurgeon said:

> This is beyond all others "The Psalm of the Cross." David and his affliction may be here in a very modified sense, but, as the star is concealed by the light of the sun, he who sees Jesus will probably neither see nor care to see David.
>
> Before us we have a description both of the darkness and of the glory of the Cross, the sufferings of Christ and the glories that shall follow. Oh for grace to draw near and see this great sight! We should read reverently, putting off our shoes from off our feet as Moses did at the burning bush, for if there be holy ground anywhere in the Scripture, it is in this psalm.

In the centuries since David wrote this psalm, countless other songs have been written to try and capture the majesty and horror of Calvary. But David's hymn rises above all, not only because it was divinely inspired, but also because it expressed realities in advance of their occurrence. His amazing words anticipated the most remarkable event in human history—the sacrifice of the Son of God.

David, however, did not fully understand the depths of which he wrote. His experiences, which prompted his words, were merely the shadows of which Christ's experiences would be the substance. Now, with the events of the cross firmly established in history, we look back with clarity. We look back with understanding. But, even more, we look back with awe. We know who Jesus was (and is). We know what Jesus did, and why. We know what crucifixion looked like in reality, and try to appreciate the depth of love that would cause Christ to embrace that cross—and caused the Father to send His Son on that anguished mission of rescue. It is more than the evidence of God's hatred of sin; it is the validation of God's love for guilty sinners. It is the revelation of the depth of God's concern for our sin—and the willingness of Christ to be broken and to have His heart broken in order to redeem us from our sin.

In the eighteenth century, the great hymnist Charles Wesley tried to capture the awe of David's psalm with a hymn of his own, proclaiming the song of saving grace:

> *He left His Father's throne above*
> *So free, so infinite His grace—*
> *Emptied Himself of all but love,*
> *And bled for Adam's helpless race:*
> *'Tis mercy all, immense and free,*
> *For O my God, it found out me! . . .*
> *Amazing love! How can it be,*
> *That Thou, my God, shouldst die for me?*

Final Thoughts

The LORD is near to the brokenhearted
And saves those who are crushed in spirit.
—PSALM 34:18

L ife in a fallen world is often unfair, usually difficult, and occasionally paralyzing. It is the burden of brokenness that seems to never find relief, but desperately needs it.

The great comfort for the child of God is that we do not face this kind of world alone. The psalmist assures us that "The Lord is near to the brokenhearted." He is both engaged and involved. He knows, sees, and cares about all that we face, and He is there to help us in our time of need. Christian musician Twila Paris put it this way: "Oh, how He longs to hold in His arms / Every heart that is breaking tonight."

It's true. The Father who has promised to never leave us or forsake us, the Son who has promised to be with us always, and the Spirit who is so involved that He actually takes up residence in our lives have promised themselves to us. So,

When your heart is breaking, the Lord is near.

When your spirit is crushed, He is ready to rescue you.

In a world filled with pain, He is the only answer for every heart that is breaking.

Turn to Him.

He listens to the song of the brokenhearted.

Enjoy this book? Help us get the word out!

Share a link to the book or
mention it on social media

Write a review on your blog, on a retailer site,
or on our website (dhp.org)

Pick up another copy to share with someone

Recommend this book for your
church, book club, or small group

Follow Discovery House on
social media and join the discussion

Contact us to share your thoughts:

 @discoveryhouse    @DiscoveryHouse

Discovery House
P.O. Box 3566
Grand Rapids, MI 49501 USA

Phone: 1-800-653-8333
Email: books@dhp.org
Web: dhp.org